HANDBOOK

FOR PARENTS

OF CHILDREN WITH SPECIAL NEEDS

- -

A THERAPEUTIC AND LEGAL APPROACH

Jayne M. Wesler

HANDBOOK FOR PARENTS OF CHILDREN WITH SPECIAL NEEDS:

A Therapeutic and Legal Approach

Jayne M. Wesler

First Printing: September 2020

Milford, PA

ISBN 978-1-7355405-0-4

Library of Congress Control Number: 2020915937

Jayne M. Wesler, Esq., LCSW
www.weslerbooks.com
www.sgwlawfirm.com

Jayne M. Wesler, Esq., is a licensed clinical social worker and a partner in the law firm of Sussan Greenwald and Wesler. The firm's practice focuses on the representation of students with disabilities in order to ensure they receive appropriate educational services.

As a psychotherapist, Ms. Wesler has worked with children and teens in various settings, including both inpatient and outpatient individual and group therapy. As a member of multiple Child Study Teams, Ms. Wesler conducted evaluations, wrote IEP's, case-managed elementary students, high-school students, and students placed in specialized private school programs. She also developed and facilitated various psychotherapy groups.

Early in her legal career, Ms. Wesler practiced at a large New Jersey law firm where she founded the Special Education Law Section. Earlier, she served as a judicial clerk to the Hon. Clarkson S. Fisher Jr., then presiding judge of the Chancery Division for the Superior Court of Monmouth County, New Jersey.

Ms. Wesler also served as a law clerk for the Monmouth County, New Jersey, Prosecutor's Office, Appellate Division, where she did a special research project for the Monmouth County Prosecutor regarding the prosecution of cases involving repressed memory of sexual abuse. As a licensed clinical social worker and an attorney, Ms. Wesler is experienced in the fields of special education, mental health, and psychotherapy.

Ms. Wesler has presented continuing education workshops on various topics in the fields of law and mental health, including IDEIA, Section 504 Plans, and the Discipline of Students with Disabilities. She has written a scholarly paper on the Americans with Disabilities Act of 1990 and a study in conjunction with the Hon. Thomas N. Lyons, Judge of the Superior Court of New Jersey, Union County, concerning the proper treatment of cases involving litigants with mental illness.

Ms. Wesler earned her Juris Doctor degree from Seton Hall University School of Law; her M.S.W. degree from New York University School of Social Work in New York City; and her B.S.W. degree, *summa cum laude*, from Georgian Court University. She is admitted to practice in New Jersey, the United States District Court for the District of New Jersey, and the Third Circuit Court of Appeals.

TABLE OF CONTENTS

CHAPTER ONE
Nothing Succeeds Like Success.

Are you worried that your child isn't developing normally?

Does your child cry frequently after coming home from school?

Does he try to avoid going to school by saying his stomach or his head hurts? Then, on the weekend, his health improves…until Sunday evening?

Have you noticed that your child isn't keeping up with her peers in school even though you are sure she is capable?

Have you raised this issue with the teacher only to be told your child is "fine"?

Has your child begun to tantrum over doing homework?

Does he scream that he is stupid? Or, worse, that he wishes he were dead?

Are you tired of ignoring the nagging concern that your child isn't developing normally? Or that he needs a different educational program?

Has anyone ever told you to *trust your gut*?

No advice could be more perfect for raising children. Children are complicated creatures who do not arrive in neat packages with technical manuals. So how does a parent know if a child is developing normally or if they need to take action to address their child's deviation from the tried and true path?

Most kids don't follow developmental plans step by step. Every kid is a little different. Most of them are what we dub "WNL": within normal limits. But what happens when your child does not fall within these parameters? Most parents will check with their pediatrician to determine whether what their child is—or isn't—doing is normal. The trouble is, the pediatrician sees your kid for only five minutes amidst a day in which they may have twelve kids scheduled every hour, on the hour, with emergencies stuck in along the way. As a lawyer and a psychotherapist who has worked with children with special needs for decades, I've seen a lot of children whose pediatricians missed the early warning signs that these children had special needs. One reason may be that pediatricians may not know the comprehensive nature of both state and federal law which exist to help remediate just those types of needs and how their patients actually fit into those categories.

That is why I have written this book: to assist you in confronting any concerns you have about your child's development and in finding help through assessments, commonsense techniques, and steps you can take to obtain an appropriate educational plan which will provide your child with the tools to succeed. I will stick with that sage advice: **Trust your gut.** If you suspect your child is different in any way, take action immediately, regardless of her age. Seek help. Remember, the first phone call is always the hardest to make.

In my decades of working with children with special needs, I have discovered the truth in the old adage, 'Nothing succeeds like success.' I don't know if your kids have any of the following complaints, but parents have come into my conference rooms year after year with these typical tales of woe regarding their children:[1]

- Liam has always struggled to meet academic goals. Now he has begun to act out in school.

- Isabella is very anxious every morning before school. She complains she has a stomachache and cannot go to school. On Saturday and Sunday, she is miraculously cured, only to have the malady return on Monday morning.

- Noah is in the third grade and can't read, but every time I ask his teacher about it, she says he's doing fine.

- Brian is an eleven-year-old boy with agenesis of the corpus callosum. He has already undergone two neurosurgeries and the surgeon has recommended a third neurosurgery.

- Geoffrey is a ten-year-old boy who is the size of a sixteen-year-old. He is severely autistic, does not speak, and wears diapers. He does not sleep through the night and wanders the house. The parents have had to install locks out of his reach to keep him from eloping.

- Grace is a brilliant and beautiful sophomore who is enrolled in all advanced placement classes. Her after-school and weekend schedules are filled with demanding

---

[1] These case studies are merely representative of the thousands of cases which have come through my offices over the years.

3

extracurricular activities at which she excels. Yet suddenly and without warning, Grace was unable to get out of bed one morning. Depression hit her swiftly, and hard. At first, the school district was understanding. After a few weeks, however, the school completely forgot about this teen and stopped sending work home for her to do.

In my experience, it is better to face such issues head on and deal with them. The solution is to 1) obtain accurate assessments so you understand the cause of your child's challenges; 2) obtain a first-hand understanding of your, and your child's, legal rights; 3) obtain all the information you need about who's who in your school district and how they can each help you; and 4) learn what to do if you run into opposition.

For many years, I heard approximately 15-20 stories a week from new clients calling with the most confounding and difficult problems. The examples go from students who appeared to have behavioral problems when they really could not hear well or communicate their needs, students with anxiety disorders being labeled as autistic and placed in self-contained classrooms with kids who really were on the spectrum, to students who had been classified as Cognitively Impaired when they really had a reading disorder (dyslexia). Our school systems are charged with many tasks and they make a lot of mistakes. For virtually every parent who came into my office and retained my counsel, there was a solution for their child. At the end of a case, my clients would often exclaim to me, "I have a new kid on my hands!" It was evident that nothing else could give a parent as much joy or happiness as seeing their child achieve the promise of that old adage, "Nothing succeeds like success."

As a lawyer, psychotherapist, and former Child Study Team member who practices exclusively on behalf of children with special needs, I have helped hundreds, if not thousands, of parents obtain educational programs which led to their child's success. In this book, I will share information with you from federal and state law, federal and state regulations, psychotherapeutic techniques, and my experience so that you, too, can change the trajectory of your child's life. If you use the techniques, tools, and knowledge I provide to you, you can and will obtain successful programs for your child to help her succeed in school—the sooner, the better.

If you learn and implement two or three of these ideas, you may know much more about your child's legal rights and how to obtain good educational programming for him. If you apply six, seven or eight of these suggestions, you may literally change the course of your child's life. If you are able to apply all of them, you may transform your child's life into one which is an amazing success story which you may not even be able to comprehend at this moment.

These principles are ideas that not only lawyers, psychotherapists or educators can apply. You yourself have the capacity to apply them. When you are done reading and implementing the knowledge and techniques, you will have a better educational program for your child and the tools to help your child achieve success.

As you turn the page and begin the next chapter, recognize this isn't a collection of ideas that worked only for me as an attorney and psychotherapist, or just for the clients on my caseload. As you apply these principles and techniques, you will learn about your child's strengths and weaknesses, how to remediate the weaknesses, how to obtain the proper instructional strategies, modifications and accommodations he requires, and how to handle yourself through the thick and thin of the journey. This will promote not only your child's welfare, but you and your family's health and well-being.

CHAPTER TWO
If you suspect a problem, start your planning immediately, no matter the age of your child.

1. My child is only an infant. Isn't it too early to think about his education?

No! Babies and young children may be eligible to receive services from a federal program called Early Intervention ("EI"). EI provides services and supports to babies and young children who are developmentally disabled. If your child is eligible, these services and supports would be designed specifically for your child's individual needs and might include speech therapy, physical therapy, occupational therapy, or developmental intervention.

To find out whether your infant or toddler is eligible for EI, you should go to the CDC website and click on your state to find a program in your area. The link to that site is https://www.cdc.gov/ncbddd/actearly/parents/states.html#t extlinks

Once you have identified a contact, reach out to that program via telephone or email and advise them that you have concerns about the way your child is developing and you would like your child to be evaluated to see if she is eligible for Early Intervention programs and services. You do not need a doctor's referral. You will need to describe the specific areas in which your child may have a developmental delay.

2. Although I suspect my baby or toddler is not developing normally, my pediatrician says he's fine. Shouldn't I wait?

Here's where I reiterate that sage advice: **Trust your gut.** Many parents feel a sense of relief when their pediatrician tells them not to worry. Unfortunately, I've had a lot of parents end up in my office years after such a response when their initial concern proved valid. It may be that the pediatrician made a mistake, or it may be that the pediatrician just did not put two and two together to come up with an appropriate conclusion. Pediatricians are not likely to be familiar with laws that identify, protect and provide for children with special needs. Therefore, they could easily give advice that is meant to be reassuring but ends up diverting a parent's legitimate concerns.

3. What kind of planning could I do before my child's first birthday?

If your child shows signs of any kind of developmental delay from birth to age three, you should immediately follow the steps outlined above to obtain an evaluation through Early Intervention. By the way, the Early Intervention program in your area may be run by an entity with a different name, so don't be thrown off by that. The sooner you contact EI, the better. Early Intervention helps infants and toddlers improve their abilities and learn new skills, and may even help erase any trace of a developmental disability. They provide services until the child's third birthday.

Years ago, before autism and its treatment were well understood, a New York City mother hired a young doctoral student to provide a new therapy to her young daughter who had been diagnosed with autism. At times during the therapy, the mother worried she was doing the wrong thing. The new therapy seemed harsh and family members criticized her. But the mother wanted a cure, so she stuck it out. By the time that little girl entered Kindergarten, she was no longer diagnosable with autism. That therapy is now well-known as discrete trial therapy ("DTT") and that young doctoral student was Bridget Taylor, now a renowned psychologist and expert in behavior analysis and effective interventions for children with autism. The mother told her poignant story in <u>Let Me Hear Your Voice</u>, available on Amazon.com.

It is a remarkable story. Your story may not be so extreme, but it does provide hope and inspiration to you, the reader, that you, too, can find success for your child.

4. What kind of planning could I do before my child turns three years old?

When your child is two years and eight months old, you may contact the Child Study Team ("CST") in your school district[2] for a full evaluation to determine his eligibility for special education and related services.[3] If your child is receiving EI services, EI should contact the CST in writing to notify them. Your school district is obligated to review that request and respond within twenty days whether it is spring, summer, fall or winter.

---

[2] Always keep a running record of your interactions with your school district. Make sure to include names, dates, and other specific details. The rule of thumb here is, if it isn't written down, it didn't happen. Lawyers often use a technique called a memorializing letter which is discussed in Chapter 3.
[3] Please see explanation of Child Study Team in Chapter 4 and more information on special education and related services, above.

The next step would be for the district to hold an evaluation planning meeting. At that meeting, you, as the parent, are part of the team to review all the information about your child and to determine whether the evaluation should go forward.[4] The team then decides what types of evaluations should be done. The school district typically does three basic assessments: a) a psychological assessment; b) an educational achievement assessment; and c) a psychosocial assessment. With a preschool child, the school district might also perform a speech-and-language assessment. At the meeting, the school district will list these assessments in a written evaluation plan. They will then ask you for your consent to perform the evaluations. Parents have to provide written consent to the school district so it may commence with the assessments. If you have requested the evaluations, you should sign the consent without delay.

Once you have signed the consent to evaluate, the school district has ninety (90) days in which to complete the evaluations, prepare evaluation reports, provide them to you so you have ten days to review them, then meet with you at an eligibility conference prior to your child's third birthday. In my experience, the school district frequently does not provide the reports to the parents with a full ten days to review. So long as you have enough time to read the reports and prepare for the meeting, my advice is not to complain about it. While the failure to provide the full ten days to review is an actual breach of federal and state law, this could be the least of your worries and the only remedy is to delay the meeting. That will not serve your child well.

---

[4] See Chapters 9 and 11 for what to do when the school district refuses your requests.

At the meeting, if the CST finds your child eligible for special education and related services ("ESERS"), it is the school district's responsibility to develop an Individualized Education Plan ("IEP"), and put that plan into place no later than your child's third birthday. You would need to sign the IEP saying that you agree with it and with the school district's provision of services.

You and your EI team and your local school district CST can do very significant assessments, planning and provision of services in the years from birth to three years old. If your child is exhibiting any signs that she may have any type of challenge or developmental delay, even if she is not receiving EI services, do not delay in seeking high-quality assessments. That is the only evidence-based way to make an accurate diagnosis. In the next pages, I will discuss all you need to know to obtain proper assessments and services so your child can be successful. Don't wait! You might regret that decision for the rest of your life.

5. What kind of planning could I do before my child reaches the age of compulsory education?

Virtually every state in the United States of America has compulsory education for all students from their sixth birthday through their sixteenth birthday. However, for children with learning differences, the federal and state law wisely mandates that they can receive an IEP, if they are ESERS, from their third birthday through the end of the school year in which they turn twenty-one.[5] Remember to **trust your gut**. If your child is

---

[5] Massachusetts actually extends that window through the end of the year in which the student turns twenty-two (22).

struggling with any type of learning or developmental milestone, reach out to the CST in writing and ask for a full CST evaluation.

6. My school district does not have a kindergarten. Shouldn't I just wait until my child is in the first grade before I contact them? What can I do?

The early elementary years offer a critical opportunity for academic and social development of children. The sooner a challenge is understood and addressed, the better it will be for your child. For instance, there is a saying in education that, *from kindergarten through third grade, a student learns to read. Thereafter, the student reads to learn.* If a student is not proficient in reading by the end of third grade, he will begin to grow increasingly frustrated when the pace picks up in the fourth grade and he is left behind. Even though many children with dyslexia, a reading disorder, are intelligent, they believe that they are stupid because their pace of academic achievement is not on par with that of their peers. At that point, they begin to feel inadequate. They begin to voice their frustration, often saying, "I'm stupid" or the more dire "I wish I were dead." Left unattended, a specific learning disability such as dyslexia can lead to the development of emotional or even behavioral difficulties.

One such case stands out in my mind. A married couple came to my office on behalf of their sixteen-year-old son. He had been acting out in school for some duration and the district had finally notified the parents that they were planning to place him in a private school for students with behavior problems. The parents were alarmed that the district was taking such action. While the idea of a private school placement might sound desirable, a school for kids with behavior problems might be, as one student told me himself, "the last stop." When I asked,

12

"The last stop before what?" he answered me with a somber look: "Jail." Needless to say, the parents wanted their son to stay in their local high school and, after consultation, hired me to achieve that goal. In reviewing the huge stack of this young man's school records, I had drilled all the way down to first and second grade. There, before my eyes, was the root of the problem. This young man, as an elementary student, had exhibited the signs of a reading disorder. I then found old evaluations with very clear data indicating such a disorder existed. How the school district failed to pick up on it, I could not answer. Unfortunately, this was a case where the young student's clearly-identifiable reading disorder went un-remediated and he developed emotional problems and behavioral difficulties on top of that. While I was able to develop and obtain an excellent outcome for the young man and the family, no one could go back and restore all those years of schooling and all those missed opportunities to that young man. His potential had gone unfulfilled.

It is for this very reason that I am writing this book so that you, the reader, can avoid this type of invisible sinkhole; so that you can learn the law and the techniques to discover how your child learns and how to obtain a program that will provide him or her with the tools to achieve success.

7. What are the normal developmental milestones for an infant? For a child ages one to three years old?

Children reach milestones in every aspect of their development: social, emotional, language and communication, cognition (learning, thinking, problem-solving), and movement and

13

physical development. Numerous resources are available so you can familiarize yourself with these milestones.[6]

8. What could I hope to get before the age of compulsory education?

There are many resources, services, modifications, accommodations, types of instruction, and related services[7] available for children from birth through the age of six. Should your child be in need of them, the sooner they are provided, the more helpful they may be.

9. When does my school district become responsible?

School districts may be responsible for providing IEP's to children who are ESERS as early as the child's third birthday.

10. My child does not seem slow, so how could she need special education?

There are several different categories in the federal and state special education law. Many learning challenges are not readily apparent and require skilled assessment to pinpoint the exact issues facing your child. The classification categories are:

- Auditorily Impaired
- Autistic
- Behaviorally Impaired

---

[6] See www.cdc.gov ; www.marchofdimes.org; www.developingchild.harvard.edu ; and the National Library of Medicine at www.nlm.nih.gov .
[7] "Related Services" is a statutory term of art and includes various types of therapies and assistance. Read on.

- Cognitively Impaired (mild, moderate, severe)
- Communication Impaired
- Deaf/Blindness
- Emotionally Disturbed
- Multiply Disabled
- Orthopedically Impaired
- Other Health Impaired
- Preschool Child with a Disability
- Socially Maladjusted
- Specific Learning Disability
- Traumatic Brain Injury
- Visually Impaired

You might wonder how on earth a learning challenge in these categories could go undetected. You would be surprised how often that occurs.

11. What is special education?

"Special education means specially designed instruction, at no cost to the parents, to meet the unique needs of a child with a disability, including—(i) instruction conducted in the classroom, in the home, in hospitals and institutions, and in other settings; and (ii) instruction in physical education." IDEA Sec. 300.39.

That is the simple definition, but it becomes more complicated as we look at the wide variety of "disability" and each student's needs. That can lead to disagreement over classification and programming, but we will confront that in Chapters 9 and 11.

Remember, too, that the phrase "at no cost to the parents" is very misleading. Parents almost always put money into their child's education, and there is usually disagreement between a knowledgeable parent and the school district. That is because the school districts often try to provide only what they have or want to and not what the child needs. And after all, what parent doesn't want to provide help to their own child? So, we give, and we pay. And that's okay.

12. What are related services?

Related services are any services provided to a student with a disability when required for the student to benefit from the educational program. That may include behavioral intervention; counseling; medical services; occupational therapy; physical therapy; speech-and-language services; school nurse services; and transportation.

13. How does a child become eligible for special education and related services?

When a child between the ages of two years, eight months and prior to high school graduation shows signs of special needs, someone—a parent, a teacher—refers her to her CST for evaluation. An evaluation planning meeting determines which evaluations will be conducted. Once those are done and reviewed, the parents and the CST meet for an eligibility conference. If the child meets the criteria for one of the special education categories, the child will be classified as ESERS.

CHAPTER THREE
Obtain Good Counsel.

1. Isn't that self-serving?

Do you think it's self-serving when your dentist recommends a check-up every six months? Of course not! Your dentist is a professional who chose his profession because he has a deep desire to help his patients maintain a healthy mouth. We know that a healthy mouth is also a healthy body. So it turns out to be good advice.

My recommendation to obtain good counsel comes from the same desire to help. There are age-old proverbs about seeking good counsel: "Plans are established by seeking advice; so if you wage war, obtain guidance." Proverbs 20:18. Another version of that same passage says: "Plans succeed through good counsel; don't go to war without wise advice." It is sound advice which I have followed all of my life whenever I have had to make important choices. As an attorney who practices exclusively in the area of special education law, I am writing this book to help you navigate an unfamiliar system. This book contains a great deal of information that can help you when you are confronted with significant decisions about your child's education. In my experience, a consultation with a knowledgeable attorney can provide you, first, with the relief of knowing that there are answers to the questions you have and, second, options to obtain solutions to your and your child's problems.

2. Why would I need an attorney?

There are several reasons you might need an attorney:

- To get answers from a trusted, objective source
- To get a succinct recitation of the law as it applies to your child
- To learn about what particular pitfalls you might face in your specific circumstances
- To obtain an outline of what the attorney herself would do in your case
- To get connected with good experts
- To avoid making an inadvertent blunder in your case that could limit your options
- To obtain the correct program for your child when your school district is not providing it
- To guide you through a hearing or a trial
- To appeal a decision by a hearing officer or a judge

After almost every consultation I have ever had, the parent was relieved that they had come. You could see it on their faces. One mother compared her visit to my office to going to a spa. It was a quiet, safe atmosphere and she felt reassured, comforted, and thankful afterward. She was able to pour her heart out, be heard, and get intelligent and specific feedback.

3. Couldn't I just get good evaluations myself?

It is possible for parents to obtain good evaluations without seeking the advice of an attorney. You need to be open-minded to seeking someone out of network and not allow your choice to be driven solely by your insurance, if that is financially possible. See Chapter 7 for more on how to obtain a good evaluation.

4. I am afraid of backlash if I get an attorney.

Many parents raise this concern when they retain my law firm. Maybe they have other children in the school system and they are worried that the staff will be angry and will retaliate. Or they think the school district will somehow seek to punish them for hiring a lawyer. Here's what I tell them. In my experience, the reverse is usually true. First of all, only a select few will know that you have hired an attorney. That is usually the administrator who oversees the provision of special services, perhaps the principal of the school your identified child could or does attend, and the CST. Second, upon retention of legal counsel, any good school district will immediately look at your child's records to ensure they are compliant with the law. That should help, not harm.

Prior to a meeting I had with a young mother, I had arrived in the central office of the school her daughter attended. Her daughter was eleven years old, intelligent, classified as Multiply Disabled, and we were seeking an out-of-district placement in a private specialized school. It was a cold winter day. I arrived first and the secretary kindly took my coat. When the mom came in, the secretary came out and took her coat as well. The mom's eyes grew wide in surprise and disbelief as this cordial behavior was a complete one-eighty from the way the district had been treating her. Remembering her concern, I smiled gently at her. Having an attorney had definitely made a difference in how she was treated—a very positive one. As that case unfolded, I was able to secure the private specialized placement we sought for her daughter, complete with transportation. She went on to thrive there, and the mom had "a new kid" on her hands.

5. What does it mean to ghost write?

Ghost writing means the real author is invisible, and that person writes the material for another person who is the named author. Attorneys might choose to do this for their clients in the beginning of a case in order to prevent the client from making costly mistakes and to maintain a more pleasant relationship between the parties. School districts have lawyers on retainer and they frequently seek legal counsel. Why should a parent not have that same right? Parents also have the right to keep such communications private, and ghost writing is one way to do that. I personally have conducted whole cases in this manner, and those cases generally settle very well. The school district administration was likely aware that the parents had legal counsel simply by the steps the parents were taking. It was also obvious that the school district had sought and obtained the advice of its attorney. But the disagreement was resolved in a more civilized, more pleasant and agreeable way by the use of ghost writing.

6. Can't we just have the pediatrician write recommendations?

You could, but my advice is, Don't do it! Pediatricians often want to help their patients. They will often write some kind of prescription for special education services at the behest of parents. In my experience, those prescriptions are not only worthless, they may prejudice your case against you.

Pediatricians are not experts in the areas from which classification arises. Pediatricians are experts in the branch of medicine that deals with the care of infants and children. But pediatricians are not specialists, and if your child shows detectable signs of a disability, your pediatrician is likely to send you to a specialist.

Experts render educational recommendations after a thorough evaluation. A recommendation scrawled on a prescription pad, with no supporting evidence or rationale, is a glaring sign to your school district that you asked your pediatrician to write the prescription. While that may not always be accurate, it will have the same affect.

This does not mean you should never seek recommendations from your pediatrician. If your pediatrician feels strongly that your child should be referred to the CST, should have a particular evaluation by the CST, or should have a particular type of special education or related service, then he should send a signed and dated letter to the school district. The letter should state his recommendations and the relevant supporting data with specificity.

7. Evaluations are expensive. Can we choose someone for whom my insurance will pay?

In choosing an expert to evaluate your child, decisions driven by insurance can spell disaster. An expert evaluation is a baseline evaluation when it is critical to discover, pinpoint and understand how your child learns academically, socially, and emotionally; how she performs her activities of daily living; how she moves through her day and her world. It is critical to get this right or nothing you do afterward will be correct. Think of it in a medical model. If you had excruciating pain in the lower right quadrant of your abdomen, you would probably go to the emergency room. The first thing the ER doctor would likely do is an examination followed by a full battery of tests to determine what is causing the pain. Imagine for a moment that the ER doctor is not trained in all areas of medicine and has little experience. She does not know what tests to use and she diagnoses you with gastroenteritis and sends you home, where your appendix bursts and you die from peritonitis. Not the outcome you were looking for, right?

I believe very strongly in getting good evaluations. I have always felt that way and I empathize with parents who have a difficult time affording the evaluations.[8] For that reason, I relented once when a parent was begging to use the in-network professionals and I recognized one of the experts' names. It is a mistake I will never make again. I had seen and read several of this man's evaluations over the years and they were pretty good. If he would do such an evaluation for my new client and their insurance would cover the cost, it was all good. Unfortunately, this expert proved unreliable in almost every aspect. I had to chase after him to get him to do a school observation, to schedule and perform the testing, and to write an appropriate report afterward. It was a terrible experience for me as a professional. Why did I have to babysit him and whip him to do his job? For the parent, it ended up costing them more money because I had to force this expert to do everything, and he did not do it well. We ended up with a lousy report. As a litigation attorney, I used the lousy report and my legal knowledge and skills to obtain an appropriate[9] program for this child. But the parent acting alone would not have had the same

---

[8] The cost of private evaluations varies and insurance will often cover at least part of the cost.
[9] "Appropriate" is a good word in special education. It means the program is designed for your child's unique needs and to help her make progress and derive meaningful educational benefit from her program.

outcome and would not even have known that the report was subpar.

8. I've heard my school district is responsible for an Independent Expert Evaluation. Can we ask for one?

Parents can request an independent expert evaluation ("IEE") and the district is required to provide it under certain circumstances.

A school district has broad authority to determine which evaluations its CST should perform on a particular child. School officials and CST members are considered experts in this area. Federal regulations simply state that a parent has the right to an independent IEE at public expense if the parent disagrees with an evaluation obtained by the district. However, at least one state (New Jersey) has amended its regulation to permit a parent to request an IEE only at the completion of the district's evaluations and if the parent disagrees with any of those evaluations. Part or all of the parent's disagreement may be because the district did not conduct certain assessments such as cognitive testing. In your request for an IEE, you should list the assessments you want done.

Keep in mind that, since New Jersey's regulation conflicts with the federal regulation by including the additional language "at the completion of," it is unclear whether that section can withstand a legal challenge.

When a parent makes a written request for an IEE to the district, the regulations require the district either to agree to do the evaluation, or to file for due process within ten days of the request to defend the reason they are refusing.

There are a number of rulings against parents in these cases, rendering this in my opinion a rather murky legal area. But parents can still obtain victories outside of court and in fact it is often desirable to reach agreement with your school district without escalating the dispute to a judge. That preserves the parties' relationship, keeps money in your pocket instead of going to legal fees, and offers both parent and school district an opportunity to turn a negative into a positive win-win situation.

Two other caveats involving IEE's: first, school districts usually have a cap on the cost which they will pay for evaluations; and second, they will usually present you with a list of "approved" evaluators. Before you ask (in writing, of course), you should review the district's policies, obtainable on its website, and have chosen your evaluator(s) and be ready to defend your choice. The law does not permit the district to narrow your choice to only the experts on its list, and if your evaluator has the appropriate license or credentials in her field, that should suffice with regard to "approval."

9. Why should I pay an attorney or an expert to do something for me when the school district should be doing these things anyway?

Good question. The basic answer is simply that the district has a budget and an agenda and they may disagree with what you think they should do. Instead of getting stuck fighting about that, accept that the district has a different opinion and move ahead with your own evaluator. This is not the hill on which to die.

10. Should I contact the media to put pressure on the school district?

When my clients get really wound up, they often threaten the district that they will contact the media. If they have already retained me, they know to discuss something like this with me first. I always tell them not to do it. The school district does not care if you go to the media. The district is not a stranger to publicity, both good and bad. Poor media coverage is not likely to do anything to help your case and may in fact worsen it by making the district administrators angry and more difficult to work with. Since settlements are by and large better than litigation, parents should remember to strike a balance between seeking an appropriate program for their child and hostile confrontation. There is a reason people say you get more flies with honey than with vinegar.

11. Should I contact my local politician to put pressure on the school district?

Once again, I advise against this. At times, some of my parents had already contacted their local politician prior to the date they retained me. Although I have seen letters from politicians to both parents and school districts, they are generally worthless in helping to obtain appropriate instructional education plans for children.

12. I know a school board member. Should I call them for a favor?

School board members do not usually want to get involved doing favors for their friends and neighbors. If you trust this school member implicitly, if you do not have an attorney, and you are getting nowhere, you could speak to them confidentially to see if they know anything or can give you any advice. But such a conversation could also damage your case or your relationship, so tread carefully. You would be better off seeking an initial consultation with a lawyer in this field.

13. When should I seek an attorney?

Speaking of initial consultations, the timing of your consultation with an attorney is critical. I have had wise parents come in when their child was two-and-one-half years old. They wanted to know what they were facing and get prepared in advance. I have also had parents wait until one month before their twelfth-grade daughter's high school graduation to seek help. While I was able to help that young woman and ultimately got two years of compensatory education for her at a specialized residential school, waiting till such a late date will mean missed opportunities for a more enriched and rewarding school career and later life.

14. What kind of attorney should I look for?

Please take care in picking the attorney who represents you. Look for one who is knowledgeable in the law and in special education and who has had at least five years in practice. Ask around and get word-of-mouth recommendations. If you know any CST people or special education teachers or therapists, ask them if they have ever been to a meeting with a parent's attorney, and whom they respect. The attorneys in my office all have professional and personal ties to this important area of law and are well-respected. You want someone who can understand your needs and your child's needs and who understands the nuances of the law and will fight for what is right. You also need someone who is strong enough to tell you the truth when you need to hear it. To maximize your choices, you could schedule and attend more than one consultation and choose the attorney who best meets your needs.

15. I have some legal/educational knowledge. If I help with the case, will that lower my cost?

The answer here is a clear and definite no. Lawyers have their own methods of handling cases. If it gets to the point where you have to hire an attorney, let the attorney do what she does best. Otherwise, it could actually cost you more money.

CHAPTER FOUR
Know Your Rights.

1. What are my child's educational rights?

If your child is struggling developmentally, socially, emotionally, with communication, or with activities of daily living, then you have the right to seek evaluation and services. For a child older than two years and eight months, you have the right to refer your child to your local school district CST for a full evaluation based on her presenting problems. You have the right to have those evaluations done by appropriately licensed and certified professionals, and you have the right to receive and review those reports prior to an eligibility conference.

Depending on what those reports show, your child may have the right to an I&RS Plan, a Section 504 Plan, or an IEP. Let me explain.

If your child is struggling in school, you or a staff member can refer him to the Intervention & Referral Services Committee. The members of such a committee are fluid depending on a child's needs. The I&RS Committee would meet to come up with interventions that may help get your child get back on track.

A student is eligible for a Section 504 Plan if he has a physical or mental impairment that substantially limits one or more major life activities. Let me explain by example: take a student who has a fatal allergy to peanuts. That is a physical impairment. If exposed to the allergen, the fatal allergy would cause anaphylaxis, which is an acute allergic reaction that can cause a skin rash, nausea, vomiting, difficulty breathing, shock and death. Such a reaction interferes with, or limits, a number of major life activities, including breathing, circulation, concentration, consciousness. This type of limitation should be seen as substantial. When assessing your child's circumstances, ask yourself if you see: the impairment, the major life activity (ies), the limitation on the major life activity (ies), and whether the limitation is "substantial." If eligible for a 504 Plan, your child could have whatever reasonable accommodations he needs to access all of the district's educational programs.

A student is eligible for an Individualized Education Plan if she has a disability that adversely impacts her educational performance and she requires special education. If she is ESERS, she is eligible to have her IEP team develop an IEP for her unique needs to help her make meaningful educational progress. Pursuant to a case decided by the United States Supreme Court, the IEP must be appropriately ambitious.

2. What are his rights locally?

Generally speaking, federal and state laws are pretty similar. State laws must provide your child with at least the rights provided for by federal law, but they can go farther if the state legislature decides to do so.

One thing you can do to understand your local school district is to go onto the school district website, find the button for the Board of Education ("BOE"), and click on it. Here you will find a wealth of information, including all of your BOE's policies and procedures and the BOE meeting minutes. It can be quite eye-opening for you to read the minutes. You will find out all sorts of information, including the amount of money the BOE is spending on special education, specialized instruction, private special education schools, and transportation for special education students to those schools.

3. What rights does the state grant him?

Your child has so many rights they are too numerous to list in this book. For your purposes here, I suggest narrowing your review to your child's educational needs, and which program he is eligible for.

4. What rights does the federal law provide?

The state laws which I identify in this book track the federal law for the most part. To review the federal law more fully, you can find it online as follows.

5. Where can I find the law?

To review the federal law of IDEA, the Individuals with Disabilities Education Act, visit www.sites.ed.gov. To review your state law, you can look at your state's regulations or administrative code. See www.fclawlib.libguides.com for a survey of 50 state special education laws and regulations.

6. What is special education?

To reiterate from Chapter Two:

> "Special education means specially designed instruction, at no cost to the parents, to meet the unique needs of a child with a disability, including—(i) instruction conducted in the classroom, in the home, in hospitals

and institutions, and in other settings; and (ii) instruction in physical education." IDEA Sec. 300.39.

That is the simple definition, but it becomes more complicated as we look at the wide variety of "disability" and each student's needs. That can lead to disagreement over classification and programming, but we will confront that in Chapters 9 and 11

Remember, too, that the phrase "at no cost to the parents" is very misleading. Parents almost always put money into their child's education, and there is usually disagreement between a knowledgeable parent and the school district. That is because, in my experience, the school districts often try to provide only what they have or want to and not necessarily what the child needs. Budgets often factor into decision-making even though that is illegal.

7. What is classification?

When a student is found eligible for special education and related services, that is their federal classification category: ESERS. State classification is a label we give students to tell us at a glance what their predominant learning challenges are. States have broken down the federal ESERS classification into more specific categories.

8. How will I know if my child is ESERS?

Most likely, either you will have your own concerns or your child's teacher will raise concerns with you. That is how the process of determining your child's eligibility usually begins. From there, either you or the teacher can refer your child to the CST in writing. Unless the concerns are very mild and you would like to try an **I&RS** Plan first, I suggest writing to the Director of Special Services. Get his or her name and specific title from the school district website. Then put together a letter that looks something like this:

Date

Dear Director <u>Last Name</u>:

Please accept this correspondence as a referral of my <u>son/daughter</u>, <u>First Name Last Name</u>, to the Child Study Team to determine <u>his/her</u> eligibility for special education and related services.

<u>First Name</u> is __ years old and in the __ grade at <u>Name of School</u>. (Here, set forth the symptoms your child is having that evidence a potential learning challenge or special need. Don't be afraid to pile it on here. You want to convince the District to do the evaluation. For instance: Isabella seems to be an intelligent child, but she is not learning to read on par with her peers. Her teacher has mentioned to me that Isabella should study more and read more at home, but she actually tries to read to us every night and she spends hours on her homework. I finally have to force her to go to sleep, often before her work is done. We suspect she may have a reading disorder).

For these reasons, we would like to meet with you at an evaluation planning meeting at your earliest convenience to discuss what assessments would be appropriate. We are available on (here give three dates when you can meet that are 7-10 business dates away).

Thank you and we look forward to hearing from you.

If there are two parents, have both sign. Otherwise, one signature is fine. Add your phone number(s) and address under your signature(s).

Make sure you keep a copy of the signed letter and make a note of when you sent it. This is a good time to start an organizational binder, as this may be a long journey and you will want to stay organized. That will make your life much easier.

Once the CST does the evaluations, you will meet with them to discuss whether your child meets the criteria for classification. If the district says your child is not eligible, please see Chapters 9 and 11.

9. What is an IEP?

Simply, an IEP is an Individualized Education Plan created for a student who is classified as ESERS.

But it really is not as simple as that. Educators and lawyers often refer to an IEP as a living, breathing document. It is fluid and should be able to change with a student's changing needs. It must be re-written at least annually at a meeting called an Annual Review.

An IEP must contain the following information to be compliant with the law:

By law, the IEP must include certain information about the child and the educational program designed to meet his or her unique needs. In a nutshell, this information is:

- **The PLAAFP, or Present Levels of Academic Achievement and Functional Performance.** The IEP must state how the child is currently doing in school. This information usually comes from the evaluation results such as classroom tests and assignments, individual tests given to decide eligibility for services or during reevaluation, and observations made by parents, teachers, related service providers, and other school staff. The statement about "current performance" includes how the child's disability affects his or her involvement and progress in the general curriculum.

- **Annual goals.** These are goals that the child can reasonably accomplish in a year. The goals are broken down into short-term objectives or benchmarks. Goals may be academic, address communication, social or behavioral needs, relate to physical needs, or address other educational needs. The goals must be specific and measurable.

- **Special education and related services.** The IEP must list the special education and related services to be provided to the child or on behalf of the child. This includes supplementary aids and services that the child needs. It also includes modifications to the program or supports for school personnel, such as consultation, training, or professional development, that will be provided to assist the child.

- **Participation with nondisabled children.** The IEP must explain the extent to which the child will participate with nondisabled children in the regular education class and other school activities. The rule is that a classified student should participate with her non-disabled peers to the maximum extent appropriate.

- **Participation in state and district-wide tests.** Most states and districts give achievement tests to children in certain grades or age groups. The IEP must state what

34

modifications in the administration of these tests the child will need. If a test is not appropriate for the child, the IEP must state why the test is not appropriate and how the child will be tested instead.

- **Duration, frequency, provider, and location.** The IEP must state when services will begin, how often they will be provided, where they will be provided, who will provide them, and how long they will last.

- **Transition service needs.** Beginning no later than the child's fourteenth birthday, the IEP must address the courses he or she needs to take to reach his or her post-school goals. A statement of transition service needs must also be included in each of the child's subsequent IEPs.

- **Needed transition services.** Beginning no later than the child's sixteenth birthday, the IEP must state what transition services are needed to help the child prepare for moving on to post-secondary education, training, or employment.

- **Age of majority.** Beginning at least one year before the child reaches the age of majority, the IEP must include a statement that the student has been told of any rights that will transfer to him or her at the age of majority. (This statement would be needed only in states that transfer rights at the age of majority.)

- **Measuring progress.** The IEP must state how the child's progress will be measured and how parents will be informed of that progress.

You can read more about IEP's at this website:

https://www2.ed.gov/parents/needs/speced/iepguide/index.html

An IEP terminates when a student is no longer ESERS (eligible for special education and related services), when the student graduates from high school, or at the end of the school year in which the student turns twenty-one.

10. What is a Section 504 Plan?

A Section 504 Plan is a plan of reasonable accommodations given to a student[10] who has a physical or mental impairment that substantially limits one or more major life activities. School districts are responsible for providing students with disabilities equal access to district-sponsored educational and noneducational (extracurricular) programs. If the student with a 504 Plan requires accommodations to do so, then the district is required to provide those accommodations in a written, legally enforceable plan.

What does that mean? Let's use the same example we used earlier. If your third-grade child has a fatal allergy to peanuts and tree nuts, his 504 Plan might include placement in a peanut-free classroom and storage of epi pens in the classroom, the central office, the nurse's office, and either attached to the student, or in a go-bag which previously-delegated staff hand off to one another throughout the day. Those are minimal accommodations for a fatal allergy. Most of the 504 Plans which I have gotten are much more comprehensive.

---

[10] A Section 504 Plan is also applicable in other settings.

11. What can I do to obtain a plan for my child?

Keep a journal of any interactions you have with the teacher(s) and the evidence you have which indicates what incidents and events have occurred that demonstrate your child is eligible for a plan. Include names, dates, times, and details. See Chapters 6 and 7 about how to go forward with specific and appropriate requests.

12. What can I do if my school district disagrees?

Remain calm. If you get a verbal disagreement, ask that staffer to put the refusal in writing. Be polite. And see Chapters 9 and 11.

13. Which plans are legally enforceable?

Section 504 Plans and IEP's are legally enforceable. I&RS plans are not.

14. What if it's summertime and school is closed when my child needs help?

You know that old saying, "If I had a dollar for every time…"? Well, if I had a dollar for every time a CST member or school administrator told a parent that "It's summer time and we don't work in the summer; come see us in September," I would have a nice bundle of cash.

My response to all of those parents is that the federal and state law is not a red carpet that gets rolled up and put away until the school district stars are ready to re-enter the galaxy in September. Nope. The law stays in full coverage and working order, even when the CST is at the beach. Every single time-sensitive notification requirement remains effective. Every testing deadline is still active. Even if it is harder to reach the staff and get some attention, the law requires adherence to the deadlines for notification, response, and testing. That is one reason why it is so important to get started as soon as possible, so you do not have to try and start the evaluation process in the summer. It also demonstrates why it is so important to put things in writing. Remember, in the school district's eyes, if it wasn't written down, it didn't happen.[11] So remember my Rule to Record and write it down.

---

[11] Not every school district or every school staffer behaves this way, of course. But I have seen enough of this amnesia that it constitutes my "rule to record."

CHAPTER FIVE
Know Who's Who in Your School District.

1. Why do I need to know this?

It is important to know who does what in your school district so you will know whom to approach with questions when you have them. It's also important to know who the players are on "your" team and what services you can expect them to provide to you and to your child. You want to be acquainted with their particular training and positions so it will help you navigate the system and pinpoint the staff who can help when you need it.

2. My child's teacher (or aide) is my next-door neighbor. Does that help?

Many of my clients have had a teacher or a paraprofessional aide who has funneled them a great deal of information that they would not normally have received. School district staff, particularly administration, can be closed-mouthed about a lot of things, including your child's performance and programs the school district could offer (if only you knew about them). These blessed friends have helped many parents because they knew in their hearts it was the right thing to do. That's why, even though I eventually knew about the information the person had provided, I never divulged that person's identity to the school district, nor would I ever have called them as a witness at a trial. We never want to throw that person under the bus!

However, just because you live next door to a staff member or you know them from a town organization does not mean they will be willing, or able, to help you get your child appropriate services. First, you might want to follow the traditional chain of command which I set forth here in this book. Save the neighbor or friend or school board member for an unusual circumstance, unless they approach you first. Even then, proceed only with caution. They may have their own agenda or axe to grind.

3. Who is in charge of special education?

Every school district has a person designated to oversee special education and related services. That person is charged with the duty to seek out, locate, and evaluate all children who are suspected of having a disability which may entitle them to receive special education and related services.[12] They must also ensure that all classified children in the school district are getting appropriate educational services and that all of the Child Study Team[13] and special services staff comply with federal and state guidelines.

Titles for this staff member vary by state and school district. The title may indicate what training and certification that person has. Usually the title is "Director of Special Services" or "Director of Special Education."[14] Sometimes the person is entitled "Supervisor of Special Services" or "Coordinator of Special Services" which means they may not have the necessary certification or licensure to rise to the level of director. Sometimes school districts use someone called "Director of

---

[12] This is called the "Child Find" duty.
[13] In some states, the Child Study Team may have a different name, such as the Student Study Team or the Evaluation Team.
[14] Please note that titles vary from state to state.

Pupil Personnel Services" or even "Assistant Superintendent." That may mean their education and training is not solely in special education. You can check that out on the school district website under special services where there may be a bio on that staff member. If not, look at the board of education's meeting minutes for the date when that staffer was approved, if you can find it. That may give you the information you are looking for. You can check with your state DOE, either on its website or via a phone call. You are not required to give your name. While there are county DOE offices, I recommend calling the main state department as you are less likely to run into someone who is affiliated with your school district staff. A lot of the county people are former school district administrators, so they may be inclined to be protective of your school staff. And you can always try Google for information on particular staff.

4. Who is in charge of IEP's?

The Director of Special Services or other designated administrator is responsible for all of the IEP's in the School District. You will find his or her signature on every IEP. While the official authority for individual IEP's is designated to each student's case manager, the reality is that the director has to approve every IEP.

5. What is a case manager?

A case manager ("CM") is usually a member of the CST, either the school psychologist, the school social worker, or the learning disabilities teacher-consultant ("LDT-C"). Less frequently, school districts might assign that duty to a speech-language pathologist. The nature of the child's disability may help decide which CST member is assigned as the CM. For instance, the school psychologist or the school social worker would be better assigned to a student who is classified as emotionally disturbed as their training and education would enable them to better assist such a student. A speech-and-language pathologist, if utilized as a CM, would likely case manage the IEP of a preschool child with a disability or a student classified as Communication Impaired.

Any time a student is identified by the CST, a CM is assigned to coordinate all notifications, meetings, testing, IEP development, IEP monitoring, and communication with parents or guardians. The CM actually has a significant number of duties which are required of her by law.

6. What is the CST?

The CST is a group of specially-trained multidisciplinary staff who evaluate students to determine whether they are eligible for special education and related services. As individuals, they each do assessment in their particular disciplines, then meet together with the identified student's parents to determine eligibility, and then, if indicated, to develop an IEP.

7. What does a school psychologist do?

School psychologists are specially trained professionals with advanced graduate degrees in assessing students in the areas of intelligence, mental health, learning, and behavior. This is the CST member who will test your child's intelligence to determine their cognitive functioning, usually with the latest version of the Wechsler Intelligence Scale for Children ("WISC"). This can help identify your child's aptitude. The school psychologist can assess and monitor children's emotions and behavior.

8. What does an LDT-C do?

The LDT-C is a teacher and consultant with an advanced graduate degree who helps identify and diagnose perceptual and learning disabilities in students and who helps develop and deliver appropriate and effective educational services and programs. The LDT-C will perform appropriate assessments to determine your child's achievement. When compared to your child's aptitude, your child's achievement can help pinpoint specific learning disabilities. The LDT-C will often use the Woodcock-Johnson Tests of Achievement ("WJTOA"); less often, the Wechsler Individual Achievement Test ("WIAT"). LDT-C's should perform the entire battery of tests, but there are some times when they choose to cut corners and will administer only selected subtests. When you meet for the eligibility conference, you can discuss which tests will be used and can make sure the LDT-C will administer all of the subtests unless there is some specific reason which makes it reasonable not to do so. There are some *unacceptable* reasons which might make the LDT-C (or other CST member) limit testing. Those include the visual or auditory impairment of the student. School district CST members must have appropriate training or be qualified through their professional licensure or educational certification to test students in the student's area of disability. If you have a student who has a visual or auditory impairment and they cannot be tested with oral or print materials, the CST must test them in a mode in which they can understand and work.

9. What does a School Social Worker do?

The school social worker is a mental health professional with an advanced graduate degree who will perform a psychosocial evaluation to pinpoint any developmental, medical, familial, emotional or psychological issues your child has experienced or is experiencing. The school social worker will likely interview you and your child, if appropriate, and possibly your child's teacher. The school social worker may also administer assessment tools such as the Conners Comprehensive Behavior Rating Scale or the Behavior Assessment System for Children.

10. What does a speech therapist do?

The speech therapist or, more accurately, the speech-and-language pathologist, is a professional with an advanced graduate degree who is trained in the disorders of communication. The speech therapist will help determine whether your child is at risk of a communication disorder, will evaluate communication skills in your child, if indicated, will help develop goals and objectives for use in speech therapy if your child requires same, and will provide speech therapy to your child if she is eligible.

11. What does a physical therapist do?

The physical therapist is a professional with an advanced graduate degree who helps identify and assess students who may have difficulty accessing educational programs and services. The physical therapist will help develop goals and objectives designed to build strength, flexibility and stamina in students with physical challenges so those students can participate in their school's programs. The physical therapist also provides physical therapy as a related service inside the school building.

12. What does an occupational therapist do?

The occupational therapist is a professional with an advanced graduate degree who addresses the physical, cognitive, psychosocial and sensory components of performance, and focuses on a student's academics, play and leisure skills, social participation, self-care skills (also known as activities of daily living or "ADL's"), transition, and work skills.

13. What does a behavioral consultant do?

A behavioral consultant is a professional whose expertise lies in the assessment of behavior. We say they look at the "ABC's" of behavior: the antecedent to the behavior, the behavior itself, and the consequences of that behavior. Through skilled evaluation, which may be a functional behavior analysis ("FBA"), the behavioral consultant can work with the staff and student to develop an appropriate behavior intervention plan ("BIP") to help change negative, undesirable behaviors into positive ones.

14. What is the difference between a behavioral consultant and a Board-Certified Behavior Analyst?

A Board-Certified Behavior Analyst ("BCBA") is a professional who has obtained a graduate degree in applied behavior analysis and then obtained certification or licensure through the Behavior Analyst Certification Board. Applied behavior analysis is the study of behavior patterns to determine what type of treatment a student requires in order to help that youngster achieve appropriate behaviors. A behavioral consultant is a person who works with students to help shape and change behavior, but who has not obtained their BCBA certification. A behavioral consultant usually has a background in psychology or social work.

15. Who is in charge of 504 Plans?

Every school has to have a 504 officer who is in charge of Section 504 Plans. Often it is the school principal.

CHAPTER SIX
Join and Develop Allies.

1. How do I join with people?

Recognize who you want to have as your allies in the school district. Be actively grateful for those people and all they do. That will help your own mindset, which will influence what you do and how you do it. Try to understand their position and their challenges. Provide them with positive feedback. Ask them outright if there is any way that you could support them. Most people will respond well to being appreciated and supported. Review and follow the other techniques set forth in this book.

2. Who are the best allies?

The best allies will be your child's teachers. Teachers are often very skilled and very caring individuals who went into their career for their love of children and to help shape and grow the next generation.

Paraprofessional aides are also good allies. They have less demand on their time than the teachers and their lips are often looser. However, don't befriend the paraprofessional at the risk of alienating the teacher. And remember that the teacher is the professional in the classroom, has the responsibility for the class, and is usually more reliable in her assessments than the aide. But not always.

Sometimes the case manager will be your ally as well. CM's are highly-trained professionals. Many of them are skilled and compassionate people who want to advocate on behalf of your child. They may speak frankly with you and tell you how to best navigate the system to get what your child needs. However, that can bring them into disfavor with the Director of Special Services or other school administrator, so be aware of this potential conflict and be careful whom you trust.

3. Should I target people with the most power?

This may seem like a smart move, but anyone with lots of power has lots to lose. It's probably better to see what you can get by developing solid relationships with your child's teachers and case manager before you go higher.

4. Why can't they just do their job?

Great question!! My sociology professor in college told us that the answer to any question is, "Sex or money." I have borrowed and revised that standard response to answer many questions in special education. The answer here is, "Money or administrative convenience." School districts always have a budget, and special education may often be shifted to a lower priority than other general education items. In addition, it can be quite difficult to schedule an entire school of children. Revising that schedule with the attendant movement of teachers, related service providers, and juggling of classrooms may be a powerful incentive for an administrator to turn down requests.

"Why," you ask, "can't the CST just do their job and give my child the services he needs to be successful?" The answer is multi-layered. What kind of budget does the school district have this year? Is there a surplus or a deficit? Has the district been sued recently? Are they paying off some kind of big bill? Did they get a new football field? What kind of morals does the superintendent have? Does the superintendent have a long-term contract (very rare these days) or is she at the beck and call of the Board of Education? Does the Director of Special Services have a backbone?

Keep in mind that, just because the school staff isn't giving you what you believe your child needs, does not mean they believe they are not doing their job. They may simply disagree with you. Do not be discouraged. There is more than one way to skin a cat. At least that's what they say. I've never seen anyone skin a cat, nor do I wish to. But you get the idea.

5. I have a demanding job and little time. What are some easy, quick ways to do this?

After you have identified your potential allies, reach out via email as soon as possible. Introduce yourself and let them know you are eager to help make the school year a positive one. Ask if there is anything you can do to make that happen. Then make sure you follow up and do as they ask. Calendar to get those tasks done, and calendar to follow up with regular praise and feedback via email. If you have more money than time, offer to send in snacks or supplies. Believe me, the teachers will appreciate it. Way back when I was a CST member in an urban school district, the average teacher spent $100 on her classroom supplies. In 2018, that cost had risen to almost $500 per year.

6. I am angry at the team! Why should I do this? Shouldn't they be doing their job??

Of course, the team should be doing their job. Sometimes they do it well, sometimes half-heartedly. They make plenty of mistakes. But being angry and acting in anger will not help your child. Since that is the reason you are reading this book, focus on your anger first. Articulate on paper why you are angry. Then identify your goal. Maybe you're angry because the CST declined to classify or even evaluate your child. Maybe your goal is to get your child the services she needs. Okay, you are in the process of doing that. Keep your eyes on that goal and remember that developing good relationships with your child's teachers and other staff members will help them recognize your child, remember your child, connect him with you and your attitude, and will help facilitate an open flow of information between you. That will only help you to reach your goal of helping your child achieve success.

7. What are some easy therapeutic techniques to join with people and get them on my side?

A few techniques to help you connect with others:

First impressions are important. In <u>Contact: The First Four Minutes</u>, author Leonard Zunin advises that the first four minutes of every encounter have the most impact. During those brief moments, your companion will determine whether to continue or terminate the contact. Be mindful of this phenomenon, and make an effort to make those first four minutes meaningful. You can use the following specific practices to help.

1. <u>Project confidence</u>. One way to project confidence is to remember an old adage that many people use to help change their behavior: *Act as if.* What does that mean? Here, when first meeting the people you would like to be your allies, you just fill in the blank:

Act as if you are happy to meet them. Smile. Shake hands or wave hello.

Act as if you are interested in them. Ask how they are and really mean it. You may be surprised to find that your feelings will catch up with your behavior.

If this feels feigned or even sleazy to you, think about this. When we behave a certain way, when we go through the motions, we change the way we feel and we may even change our brains. Consider these studies:

- The act of smiling changes your mood, reduces stress and lowers your heart rate.[15] Yup, you can fake it till you make it.

- Smiling changes your brain chemistry. When you smile, the movement in your face sends a signal to the left frontal cortex of your brain. The brain responds by releasing serotonin and dopamine, also known as the "happiness chemicals," thus elevating your mood with a simple act.[16]

- Smiling changes the way others respond to you.

- Smiling makes you appear more charismatic. University of California psychology professor

---

[15] Smiling can trick your brain into happiness—and boost your health. www.nbcnews.com ; Grin and Bear It! Smiling Facilitates Stress Recovery. www.psychologicalscience.org ; Psychologists find smiling really can make people happier. www.sciencedaily.com quoting from researchers at the University of Tennessee at Knoxville.
[16] A Smile Can Change Your Brain by Carol Kinsey Goman, www.forbes.com .

Howard Friedman performed extensive research on the role that body language and nonverbal cues play in others' perception of us. *Id.* People who smile more, especially with the distinct crinkling of genuine intent around their eyes, are perceived as charismatic. *Id.*

- Finally, if you haven't noticed, when you smile at others, they usually smile back at you.

Another way to project confidence is visualization and the use of your body. Practice this by closing your eyes and picturing yourself walking toward your child's school. As you stride up the sidewalk, picture yourself growing taller. Breathe in and feel your body grow taller. Feel any tension in your body drain away. Feel your muscles relax. Take a deep breath, all the way down into your belly, then exhale deeply. Picture yourself meeting with your allies or even anyone who has been adversarial with you. Picture yourself making eye contact, standing up straight, feet hip distance apart or a little closer, and keeping your chin up. Smile. When you go into the school and meet with any of the staff, carry this imagery with you.

2. Use creativity and demonstrate caring to connect with your potential allies. Tune into their thoughts and feelings. Make eye contact. Relax your body and pay attention to the speaker so they get the impression that you are not in a hurry to go anywhere but, for this moment, you have devoted your whole attention to what they are saying. Demonstrate you are paying attention with a follow-up comment.

3. Show consideration. Demonstrate that you care about the role the teacher, aide, or case manager (or other recipient of your attention) plays in your child's school. Show you are interested in the challenges they face. Empathize and find something positive to say about their performance, their skill, their dedication. You will buoy and uplift them and they will remember that. Think of the words of William Arthur Ward: "Flatter me, and I may not believe you. Criticize me, and I may not like you. Encourage me, and I will not forget you."

4. Mirroring Body Language. Another technique to make others predisposed to like you is to consciously mirror their body language. This is a way of bonding with others and encouraging them to accept us. It's a way of telling others that we are similar, that we have the same beliefs and attitudes. Professor Joseph Heinrich from the University of Michigan discovered that the urge to mirror others is hardwired into our brains, and that in primitive times it served to make us more successful, thus increasing our chances of survival. Utilizing it today toward more modern ends is not different and perhaps just as critical.

While we unconsciously mirror the body language of others, we can do so intentionally to reap certain benefits. Practice the following, maybe first in your own mirror:

- Mirror another's facial expressions, especially women's facial expressions.

- Mirror another's body language, especially men's body language. Men mask their facial expressions and express their emotions through body language.

- Mirror the gestures and postures of the person with whom you are talking. That tells them that you agree with their thoughts and beliefs. It is also a sign of respect for the other person and will unconsciously be seen as such.

- Mirror a person's intonation, speed, use of words or phrases to build rapport. Never speak faster than another person as they may feel intimidated or pressured.

5. Catch Them Doing Something Right. This method is actually widely used in school districts and other settings in order to motivate others to do what we want them to do. It is otherwise known as Positive Reinforcement and it's very simple. It may come naturally to you or you may have to work at it in order to deliver the message with sincerity.

  Our brains are predisposed toward negativity. It's a survival mechanism that does not always serve us well in the modern industrialized world. We easily pinpoint things that others do wrong. In other words, we are easily judgmental and critical.

  You can turn that skill around. Once you do, you may find it's very enjoyable, especially once you start reaping the rewards of making others happy. Simply notice something good that your child's teacher or aide or case manager has done. Bring it to their attention and praise them for it. By doing this, you will likely see an increase in the behavior you are praising and the recipient will feel recognized, valued, and happier. This technique also works well with spouses and others. (That's a joke, people).

8. How can I get the teachers on my side?

First, get to know your child's teachers. Utilize the techniques above, and find out a little about their lives (unless they obviously don't want to discuss that with you).

Second, attend Open Houses and Teacher Conferences. These are the times the teacher has set aside to meet with you, provide you with important information on your child's progress, and to answer any questions you have.

Third, if your child requires a little more explanation than is possible at an Open House, schedule a private meeting with the teacher.

Fourth, make sure to take care of the basics. What does this teacher expect from your student and from you? Do your best to check in with your student's work daily to ensure she is meeting the basic requirements of the class. Review checklists, completed homework assignments, any classwork, tests, quizzes, or notices that she has brought home.

Fifth, communicate, through whatever method the teacher prefers. If it's easy for her, she is more likely to do it. Many teachers like to use email for parent-teacher communications. This usually works well for parents, too, as it is convenient for both parties to read and respond when they are able. It is also a good way to create or add to a "paper trail."

If your child is struggling, communication is critical. Be specific and succinct about the problem. For instance, the general rule for the amount of time a student should spend on homework is called the "Ten-Minute Rule." It means that a child should be able to complete her homework in approximately ten minutes per night per grade level. That computes to ten minutes per night for first graders, twenty minutes per night for second graders, and so on, up to two hours per night for high school students. If your child cannot finish her homework in the time allotted, you should let the teacher know. Remember the "who, what, where, when, why, and how" questions in order to give the teacher the important details. Here is a fictitious example of an email a parent might send to a teacher:

Hi, Ms. Miller:

This is Roberta Myler, Hailey Myler's mom. I just wanted you to know that Hailey really struggled with tonight's assignment. She worked so hard to sound out the directions and it took her so long to get through it that she did not understand what to do. For that reason, I re-read the directions to her and she completed the assignment as best she could. However, she also struggled to write out her answers. Are you seeing this in school? Do you have any suggestions for what to do at home?

Thank you.

You should designate a file in which to keep all of your and the teacher's emails. Remember the organizational binder I mentioned? That is an excellent resource for you. It is a good way to manage your child's educational and medical history and to keep that all-important paper trail.

Sixth, offer to support the teacher in any way possible. Does she need you to bring in cupcakes for a party? Does she need extra supplies like paper towels or wet wipes? Does she need a chaperone for field day or a field trip? Tell her she can count on you, as long as you are not overextended. You could even offer to be the class mother or father (yes, it's been done), if that would not put you on overload. Being in the classroom and on trips or in school during events can give you a lot of feedback about how your child is doing in that environment and compared to her peers. It also will bring you into contact with other school staff and you will become a known and trusted face in the school. That will be to your and your child's benefit.

9. Should I recruit the aide?

That depends on the purpose of the recruitment. You should absolutely be friendly and courteous with the aide. She—your child's aide will most likely be a female unless your child is a boy who needs help toileting or for some other reason needs a male aide—may be a source of a vast amount of unfiltered information about what really goes on in school. I have seen this occur time and time again. An aide's input is invaluable. However, do not expect that the aide has any power in the classroom or to get anything done officially. Depending on the aide, you might get a lot of attention and assistance, but keep in mind that you are really looking for an appropriate program written down in a legally enforceable document and not a series of undocumented freebies doled out due to someone's kindness and possible ignorance. Do not expect to email back and forth with the aide or to have the aide attend meetings to give input. Teachers are in charge of their classroom and of parental communications. They are responsible for developing the PLAAFP sections for IEP's in which the student's performance and progress are written. But for obtaining a largely unfettered

57

two-way avenue of communication, aides are usually the best source.

10. How can I manage my own emotions when I'm angry?

This is a tough one. I have been witness to some extraordinarily deplorable actions by aides, teachers, case managers, and school administrators. One example: the parents of a waif-like eight-year-old girl—I'll call them Bob and Ellen Baldwin[17]; the girl, Suzy—came into my office for a consultation. They brought Suzy with them as she had been suspended from school. Suzy was classified as eligible for special education and related services based on an auditory impairment. During a week of district-wide standardized testing, Suzy's teacher was reading the testing directions out loud in the classroom. Suzy was not able to keep pace with the teacher at a rate that allowed her to understand what she was supposed to do. She raised her hand to seek clarification while the teacher was talking. The teacher became so angry that she flung the manual at Suzy, striking her in the upper left arm. Suzy was so upset she asked to go to the office. The teacher refused and made her remain in the class. Suzy became so distraught that she wet her pants, and the teacher allowed her to go to the nurse. Suzy reported all the details to the nurse and the nurse notified the principal. No one notified Bob and Ellen Baldwin what had happened, and Suzy went home from school on the bus. When the principal interviewed the teacher after school, she made up a story implicating Suzy for alleged misbehavior. Suzy was suspended.

---

[17] All names and circumstances are fictitious accounts to give the reader an idea of what events do occur and how to handle them.

This story made smoke come out of my ears. It took us a while to straighten out the situation with the school district. Meanwhile, the parents and I took great care to maintain above-board attitudes and to be respectful and cordial in all our communications. That served only to highlight the barbaric nature of the teacher's actions. Ultimately, I was able to have the district return Suzy to school, but with a different teacher in a different classroom. I had the district remove the "suspension" from the child's records, and the teacher was reprimanded by the principal and compelled to undergo training on recognizing the signs of disabilities in grade-school students.

For sure, it can be quite challenging to maintain your temper when your school district is refusing to recognize or acknowledge your child's struggles, or when the district refuses to provide the kind of program your child requires to reach his potential, or when the district staff are downright hostile to you. It takes patience, determination, and practice. Unfortunately, you might get plenty of practice. Here are some basic techniques to use:

1) **Let reason rule**. Determine for yourself that, whatever the school district does, you will behave in a way that is true to yourself.

   - This reminds me of a story I heard decades ago of a man visiting his friend one evening in New York City. The men walked to the corner kiosk to buy a newspaper. The sales agent was rude to the man, who replied kindly and wished the agent a good evening. Once out of earshot, the friend inquired why the man had replied to the rudeness so kindly. The man replied, "I don't allow

59

others to dictate my behavior." There is a powerful moral in that story.

- Another great old adage to steer by is, "Don't argue with a fool. He will drag you down to his level and beat you with experience." Your school district has much experience in these matters and you are a parent. They have their ways of doing things, which you may not ever change. It makes sense to withdraw from a battle you cannot win in order to develop better plans so that, ultimately, you can win the war. Don't die on this hill!!

2) **Below your chin**. What is happening under your chin? We often ignore our bodies' signals because we are thinkers and we often stay in our heads. How is your body reacting? Has your heartrate increased? Is your breathing shallow? Do your intestines feel as if they are twisted? Are your muscles tense? Take a moment to do a mental survey of these areas. Then try this simple exercise:

- Find your feet. Are they warm? Cold? Cramped? Comfy? Just be aware of them for a moment. Then take a deep breath, all the way down into your belly. "Breathe, the belly," as my sage Chinese acupuncturist used to tell me. It oxygenates your blood and tells your vagus nerve that there is no threat, thus having a calming effect.

3) **Take notes! And kill 'em with kindness.** A very effective method which I have used requires you to maintain a pleasant demeanor and tone of voice while noting what the person is saying. If you don't know the staffer's name, ask for it. If they refuse, smile and say out loud while writing it

down, "Ok, this (man/woman) refused to give me (his/her) name. It is (time) and we are standing (note location, for example, "in the hallway just outside the front office of the Clara Boothe Elementary School.") Write what you are asking for. Then ask the person pleasantly what more can be done to answer your question or to deal with your problem. Ask if there is anyone else who would be able to help you. Maintain your pleasant demeanor and calm voice. Continue to record all the responses and be obvious (but not obnoxious) about it. The staff member may reconsider in the face of certain discovery. If not, you will have enough detail to identify this person to the appropriate supervisor as you make your way up the chain of command in search of a solution.

4) **Paper trail.** You should always maintain a paper trail of your situation and any requests you make of your school district. Keep detailed notes in a journal, or, better yet, the organizational binder (remember the "who, what, where, when, why, and how" questions and ask any that seem appropriate) and keep all correspondence and emails. I know this is frustrating!! But organization and details are very important in getting your child an appropriate program. Just do your best. It will be enough.

5) **Use visualization.** Picturing the person with whom you are angry in a foolish or absurd costume or position can help you smile and be polite. Picture them wearing a diaper or sitting on a toilet. Anything to make you smile. Or picture what you will do after this meeting or interaction that will soothe you: go for a run, have your hair cut, take a hot bath or a long shower, or have a cup of tea or coffee.

61

6) **Rewrite the ending**. Psychologists teach the concept of "learned optimism." In this theory, you learn the ability to view the world from a positive point of view. You can cultivate this talent with a little practice. Optimists expect good things to happen to them. They view setbacks as temporary challenges that they can and will overcome. Remind yourself regularly that the setbacks you now face are temporary. Picture what good things will come out of these circumstances. Brainstorm these good outcomes by writing them out, as many as you can. Picture them happening. Think of the good things you have been able to achieve for your child thus far. Understand that those achievements were the result of your efforts. Listen to the song, "Tubthumping," by Chumbawamba; "This is My Fight Song" by Rachel Platten; or other inspirational music. Don't give up.

7) **Fear**. Finally, remember that, if you lose your cool, the district has the option to escalate the encounter by calling the police or getting a restraining order against you. You wouldn't be the first parent who was no longer permitted on school district property due to aggressive or even threatening behavior. While it is not a complete rupture of the parent-school relationship (leave that to litigation!), it is very hard to repair this type of breach of trust between you and your school district.

11. Should I run for a position on the Board of Education?

Some of my clients have been members of their local board of education. They did not have to renounce their position just because they became at odds with their own school district.

However, if we had to file for due process, they did have to withdraw.

I would say this: if you want to become a member of the board of education out of your desire to make your school system a good one or other noble purpose, go ahead. We need good people who care about the students to serve in that capacity. If you want to do it because you think the special needs students are getting short shrift in your school district, go ahead and do it. That takes courage because special education has been known unofficially as the step-child of general education, and its needs, despite legal mandate, are often relegated to lower rungs of the budget.

If you want to run for the BOE just to help your own child, that is probably not a great reason. But if you feel strongly about it, go ahead and do it anyway. Be careful to whom you speak about your child's needs, IEP, or 504 Plan. The old adage is true: "Loose lips sink ships." You could inadvertently reveal a detail that could be used against you or your child. And if you have hired an attorney or plan to, please do not discuss your case with anyone other than your attorney and your spouse.

12. Once I have identified personal allies, how do I recruit them?

If you follow the other recommendations in this chapter, you will be well on your way to initiating and developing relationships with staff members who can be your allies.

13. How to communicate effectively with potential allies.

If it is summertime and you have been notified of the identity of your child's teacher or case manager, start off with a cheerful email in which you introduce yourself as your child's parent. You can share a note of enthusiasm ("We are looking forward to an exciting new year!") with the teacher. Make an offer of assistance tempered by how much time you actually have to offer. You don't want to promise something you cannot deliver.

If you are starting to develop these relationships in the middle of the year and you are already acquainted with the teacher, the aide, and the case manager, make the most of every opportunity they offer to meet with them. Use the techniques, above, which you have learned and practiced. If you follow these steps, you will likely develop a close and rewarding relationship with at least some of the staff who work closely with your child. The benefits you reap will be worth all of your efforts.

CHAPTER SEVEN
Know What to Ask For.

1. Do I just write down what I think my kid needs and ask for that?

The answer to many of these questions is, "That depends." Why is that? Because the facts of your specific situation will dictate the response. You may have a good idea what your child needs up front, but you may also be unaware of the deeper issues which cause your child to struggle. For example, if you are certain that all your child needs is placement in resource center for reading, writing and math because he has a relatively slight weakness and is easily distracted, you could go ahead and ask for that and maybe the case manager, the CST, or the Director of Special Services would give your request the green light.

The dangers here, however, are many. You may be missing your child's real issues. Even professional people who are educated and trained in the various disciplines which encompass special education miss these things. If you miss the real issues, your child will end up thinking he's stupid and feeling devalued and demoralized. It will undoubtedly affect his self-esteem and the goals which he believes he can achieve. It can eat away at any motivation he has to try harder, to try new things, to maintain friendships and outside interests. In short, missing your child's real issues can be an unmitigated disaster.

If you miss the real issues, you will not know what to ask for. You will not learn what services, accommodations, and modifications the school district must provide to your child, and which ones will help him learn to, in the words of the law, "obtain meaningful educational benefit" and gain "significant learning." Your child will be left wanting. And we don't want that. It could be the waste of his whole life.

Even if you do know exactly what your child needs, asking for it up front without any proof he needs it can put you in a quandary. What if the CST refuses to give your child the type of instruction or programming you request? You will likely have to obtain the help of a suitable expert and ultimately get recommendations once that person has completed his assessment. If you go back to the CST with your expert report three months after they turned down your first request and your expert report repeats your original recommendations, the CST will believe that you paid an expert to say what you wanted. They will accuse you of having an *idee fixe*, a fixed idea of what you wanted ahead of time and that you found an expert willing to put those recommendations on paper and sign his name to it—for a fee. You have now dug yourself into a hole.

The key here is balance. Know when to hold 'em and know when to fold 'em. Personally, I have always liked to get expert advice for any important decisions. I don't need to follow it, but at least I have the pertinent information at my disposal. As to whether you can just ask the CST for the modifications and accommodations or types of instruction you think your child needs, use your best sense of whether your CST (after all, you've made the CM, the teacher and ,the aide your close allies, right?) will give you what you are asking for. Ask yourself, What evidence do I have that my child needs these things to make his program work? If you don't have the evidence, gather it *before* you ask. If you do have the evidence and other staff will back you up, you could make your requests and see what happens.

2. My sister is a special ed teacher and she gave me some tips. Should I just follow her guidelines and ask for that?

Having a relative who is "in the business" can be a great help, or a great hinderance. It's always the same, isn't it? There are two sides to every coin. On one hand, a relative who is well-trained and experienced in special education can often spot warning signs in children even outside of their classroom. On the other hand (that pesky other side of the coin), your relative may be trained and experienced in only one area and may see only that. It's like, if you're having an ailment and you go see a surgeon, what does he tell you? You need surgery.

Another example today is that, when a kid acts out, or is a bit of a loner, or has sensory issues, suddenly he's autistic. That's because everyone knows about autism, so they see it everywhere.

Another example is the prevalence today of prescriptions for anxiety drugs. In August 2018, www.cnbc.com reported that, according to the National Institute on Drug Abuse, the number of prescriptions to treat anxiety had risen 67% between 2002 and 2015. Are Americans really that much more anxious? Or is the increase in prescriptions more about our expectations and our perceptions?

Having a relative who is experienced in special education can be a real asset. Have her attend meetings with you, if she can. Have her review reports and listen to her recommendations. But don't leave your own common sense out on the sidewalk. Utilize the same guidance here I gave you about your own recommendations. And remember: **Trust your gut.**

3. My relative is an educational professional and did an informal assessment at our recent BBQ. Should I have her write something up?

Once again, that depends. How informal was the assessment? Did she use actual tools? (I mean assessment tools, not a hammer and a chisel.) Did she do an observation of your child at the BBQ? For how many minutes? Did she observe him interacting with adults? With his peers? Communicating verbally and non-verbally? Following one- and two-step directions? Reading a paragraph? Did she ask any questions with regard to your child's comprehension of that paragraph? (This need not be obvious. A skilled evaluator can use almost any setting to conduct excellent assessments.) Is it something she can write up as an independent evaluation complete with recommendations?

You get the idea. If you need a referral to the CST, you could use your relative's informal findings and conclusions in order to make your own referral. If she is willing to make it formal and she can support all of her recommendations, you could get started with that. But if you are trying to ensure that the program is meeting all your child's needs, please consider using a professional expert.

4. Why should I get an objective professional evaluation?

The main reason to get one or more objective professional evaluations is to truly understand how your child functions, to fully understand the type of educational programming your child needs, and to be able to demonstrate those needs through objective scientific evidence. You need to know what to ask for, and you need to be able to convince the school district that your child needs it. Trust me, they can take some convincing. A good expert evaluation will be exactly what you need.

As a lawyer and a former Child Study Team evaluator, I do think there are many good CST members out there. But if it were my child, I would go for a private evaluation because, with a CST evaluation, you will get a rather brief evaluation report that is meant to get the job done. That is different than the report of a private expert evaluator whose goal is to be thorough and to leave no stone unturned regarding your child's educational needs.

5. Who could do a good evaluation?

This is what we used to call the Sixty-Four Thousand Dollar Question.[18] It depends on so many factors.

If your child is not already classified, refer her to your school district's CST. The CST has ninety days to do an initial evaluation, so get it going and sign the consent forms for any and all CST evaluations that the district wants to do.

If your child is already classified, if it has been at least two years since the previous CST evaluations, and if you have a good rapport with your CM and trust your CST, you could speak to the CM (remember to memorialize the conversation!) about

---

[18] If you don't know it, this expression means something which is not known and on which a great deal depends. It was the top prize in an American game show which was broadcast from 1955 to 1958.

your concerns and as to whether the district is willing to do the triennial evaluation sequence a little early.

If you do not trust your CST, consider getting one or more private evaluations. If you have hired an attorney or you intend to do so, please allow your attorney to direct you to appropriate experts. If you have not hired an attorney, consider the following to help you choose appropriate experts:

Do you have a good idea of your child's intellectual aptitude?

If your child's IQ is in the average range or above and she is struggling with reading, writing, or math, you should have an evaluation by an educational psychologist who can do both the achievement and the aptitude testing. That will tell you whether your child has a specific learning disability.

Does your child have any hearing impairments? Does she have difficulty keeping up with the flow of conversation? Does she have trouble differentiating conversation from background noise? If so, you may need an audiologist to test her hearing and whether she has an auditory processing disorder.

Does your child have any repetitive activities, resistance to change in daily routine, unusual responses to sensory experiences, and lack of responsiveness to others? If so, you should get two evaluations, one by a speech-and-language pathologist who will test all types of your child's communication, including non-verbal and pragmatic communication. You should also have an evaluation by a neurodevelopmental physician or a psychologist who can administer a test called the ADOS (Autism Diagnostic Observation Schedule). If your child has not been diagnosed with autism and this frightens you, think of this: it is better to confront your worst fear and find out the truth. There is a wide range of ability in children who have autism, and they can make great progress and have very fulfilling lives. But they need to have particular types of instruction, the earlier, the better.

Does your child seem to take longer to reach developmental milestones? Does she struggle with activities of daily living that are typical for her same-age peers? You should seek out a thorough psychological and educational, or learning, evaluation by someone who is well-trained in special education and who has experience with children who have developmental disabilities.

Does your child have difficulty communicating? Is his speech unintelligible to an unfamiliar listener? Find a good speech-and-language pathologist and have a comprehensive assessment.

Does your child exhibit inappropriate types of behaviors under normal circumstances? Is she plagued by a pervasive mood of unhappiness or depression? Does she have physical symptoms or fears associated with personal or school problems? Is she unable to build or maintain satisfactory interpersonal relationships with peers or teachers? Get a referral to a good psychiatrist who can assess her mental health.

Does your child have malfunction or loss of bones, muscle or tissue? You should seek out a thorough medical evaluation. Go to a medical center with a good reputation for thorough evaluations of children. A few excellent examples include Children's Hospital of Philadelphia, the Child Mind Institute in New York City, or Kennedy Krieger Institute in Baltimore, Maryland. If you find that your insurance does not cover evaluations at those institutions, you could try places like the Institute for Child Development at Hackensack University Medical Center or Goryeb Children's Hospital, both in New Jersey. If you are not close to either of these institutions, you can find similar ones near you. You may need a physical therapy evaluation as well.

Does your child have a chronic condition that leaves him with limited strength, vitality or alertness? Has your child ever been diagnosed with ADD or ADHD? Is your child on any type of medication? You could start with an evaluation by a neurodevelopmental physician and possibly a psychiatrist. Depending on the outcome, you might consider further evaluation at one of the above-referenced medical centers.

Is your child between the ages of three and five and either experiencing developmental delay or does he have a disabling condition? You need a psychologist who specializes in evaluating and treating preschool children.

Has your child suffered a traumatic brain injury ("TBI")? If so, you probably already have a neurologist. You can have that physician write a report with recommendations which you can present to the CST. However, you may need an evaluation by a neuropsychologist who can address not only the specific way your child's brain functions, but also his learning needs.

Does your child have a visual impairment? The first thing you should do is to get connected with the National Federation of the Blind in Baltimore, Maryland ("NFB"). That is a must. You will not find a more knowledgeable and dedicated group of professionals anywhere who understand what it is like to live and learn with blindness. They can help steer you in the right

72

direction. Regarding expert evaluations, you will likely need an evaluation by two experts: a low-vision specialist and an expert in orientation and mobility. Since visual impairments are low-frequency disabilities, you (or the expert) may have to travel.

Years ago, I had a significant case involving an elementary student who was blind. Most blind people have some vision, and Jack[19] was no different. For that reason, his school district refused to provide him with Braille instruction.

There are two schools of thought regarding Braille instruction. Until I met Jack, I was aware of only one: if a student has some vision, you teach him to be a print reader. Luckily for Jack, his teacher of the blind and visually impaired ("TBVI") was connected with the NFB and was well-versed in the other school of thought: when a student struggles with seeing information up close, you teach him Braille.

While luck was with Jack in the provision of a smart and resourceful TBVI, it was against him in his school district placement. The Director of Special Services in Jack's school district was one of the rudest and most recalcitrant directors I have ever met. He absolutely refused to provide Jack with Braille instruction, despite the recommendations of the TBVI.

To obtain the educational program Jack needed, we had him evaluated by a psychologist who had expertise in testing children who were blind and in developing their educational programs. We also had a low-vision expert test him to determine what kind of instruction he needed.

---

[19] Names and circumstances have been changed to provide an example of how similar cases turn out.

The answer was unequivocal. Jack needed to learn Braille. The poor kid was bent over his fifth-grade desk every day with his eyeball about four inches away from the page. Not only is it difficult to read for comprehension in such a manner, it is difficult to see with a shadow over the page and it is difficult to hold your head in that position without ending up needing a chiropractor.

To make a long story short, the Director of Special Services refused to provide the Braille instruction Jack needed and the case ended up going to trial. While having to commence litigation is fairly typical in a special education matter, actually going to trial happens in less than two percent (<2%) of these cases.

After a trial of nine days, the judge delivered the verdict. The school district had to provide Jack with Braille instruction, a list of education services to make up for their previous failures (that's called "compensatory education"), and numerous services and make-up hours with the TBVI. I could never have obtained this outcome for Jack without good expert evaluations.

6. What does a good evaluation look like?

Good expert evaluations are thorough. They usually start with a review of all your child's records (although some evaluators prefer to see the child before reviewing records). Before the expert meets the child, the expert should observe the child in school. On a date thereafter, the expert will administer the testing. You may not hear from the expert for a while afterwards. This is the time any good expert will be putting all of the information she has on your child together and will be working very hard to figure out your child's learning nuances and needs. This takes time, so do not keep calling or emailing the expert to find out when they'll be finished or—far worse—threaten them. The expert evaluator will put all of this information into a report which should end with very specific recommendations for your child's educational programming. The expert should exercise his authority in making appropriate recommendations clearly and succinctly. Writing that the child "may benefit from" something will not get you across the finish line. If the expert believes the child needs the particular programming piece, he should simply state that he is recommending it, or even strongly recommending it.

Do not be shy about telling the expert what you know about your child and how your child learns best. But once the expert works through all of the information and writes the report, recognize that the expert usually knows best. That does not mean that you cannot challenge an expert's recommendations or ask for more. But an expert with integrity will not write recommendations he cannot support.

You know you have a good report if you, like a number of my clients, can say, "That's my kid on paper."

7. I'm not an educator or a psychologist. How do I decipher these evaluations?

An expert will typically offer a follow-up meeting with the parents to review the evaluation report. You will learn a lot from the expert during this meeting. Make sure to ask all the questions you have and to take notes so you can review it later.

8. What is an intelligence test?

An intelligence test measures your child's reasoning and problem-solving abilities. It is supposed to gauge how well a student can use information and logic to answer questions and to make predictions compared to others her age.

9. What is an achievement test?

An achievement test is an assessment of developed knowledge or skill.

10. What are standard scores?

Put simply, a standard score indicates how far above or below the average score a student's performance falls. For example, the average IQ on the WISC is 100. If your student's WISC IQ score is 92, his score is 8 points below the exact average score.[20] If your student scores 115 on the WISC, his score is 15 points above the exact average score, and so on.

11. What is a relative proficiency?

If you don't know what this is, don't feel bad. I was trying a case in Atlantic City, New Jersey, one year and was cross-examining the school district's LDT-C. You may recall that the LDT-C is a learning disabilities teacher-consultant and should have an expertise in testing student achievement. That would include every facet of the Woodcock-Johnson Tests of Achievement, which is considered to be the gold standard testing instrument for this purpose.

---

[20] The Average range on the WISC is from 90-110. Therefore, this student's IQ score of 92 would be in the Average range.

So here I am in the courtroom, going through some "softball" (read: easy) questions designed to warm up this witness, who had already been qualified as an expert in educational testing. The questions went something like this:

Me: "You're familiar with the Woodcock-Johnson Tests of Achievement, correct?"

The Witness: "Yes."

Me: "And you're familiar with standard scores, correct?"

The Witness: "Yes."

Me: "And you're familiar with RPI, correct?"

The Witness: Crickets.

Imagine my surprise when he then answered, "No."

I had never expected this. The basic level of competence for an LDT-C requires him to be fully familiar with every aspect of a gold-standard testing instrument on which he has been trained and uses every working week of his professional life. You can bet the school district's attorneys (there were two against me) were not expecting it, either.

I recovered quickly and asked: "Did you just testify that you as the district's LDT-C are *unfamiliar* with RPI?"

What could he say? Of course, he said yes.

Me: "Can you tell the court what 'RPI' stands for?"

He couldn't.

Me: "You mean to tell me (grandstanding now) that you, the district's LDT-C, do not even know that RPI means Relative Proficiency Index?"

By this point, he had shrunk into himself on the witness stand and you could hear the sputtering and gasping from the district's attorneys.

Needless to say, after I ripped him with several more questions, I had him disqualified as an expert witness and proceeded to get a quick settlement agreement in favor of my client.

But back to RPI or, as you now know, Relative Proficiency Index. The relative proficiency index is a column that appears in the results of the Woodcock-Johnson Tests of Achievement. They will show your child's level of proficiency (i.e., accuracy, speed) at the level at which his peers are 90% proficient. For example, an RPI of 90/90 would mean that, at the difficulty level at which your child's peers were 90% proficient, your child would also be 90% proficient.

12. What are rating scales?

A rating scale is a common method of data collection used to gather comparative information about a specific subject. If you have ever filled out a survey in which you had to mark "Strongly disagree," "Disagree," "Neutral," "Agree," or "Strongly Agree," you have filled out a rating scale.

13. Should I expect the evaluator to alter her report?

Once the evaluator has completed her report, she will give it to you for your review. If you find any errors in the background or record review sections or any typographical errors, you should bring them to her attention and she will revise her report accordingly. Otherwise, do not expect the expert to alter her findings, conclusions or recommendations. The expert is the expert.

14. Should I ask the school district for everything the evaluator recommends?

Absolutely yes. The expert would not make educational recommendations for things she does not believe your child needs. That said, if the district agrees to provide your child with the majority of the recommended items, especially the most important ones, you could agree to such a program and then monitor how she does going forward.

CHAPTER EIGHT
Ask and Ye Shall Receive.

Let's talk about the ancient exhortation, "Ask and ye shall receive." It's really a simplified version of a scripture verse: "Ask and it shall be given you; seek, and ye shall find; knock, and it shall be opened unto you." There are at least twenty-eight translations of that passage, but the message in all of them is clear: Go for it!! And be persistent.

How, you might ask, does a scripture verse fit into this handbook? Maybe you're not Christian. No problem. The advice is for all people of every race, ethnicity, religious belief, gender, age, ability, sexual orientation, and sex. I used the example to demonstrate that, from time immemorial, you have to ask for something in order to get it. The answer is not always an immediate yes. It might be yes, it might be no, it might be 'later.' The answer might be, 'It depends.' It depends on where you are in this process. It depends on the age of your child. It depends on whether you are acting as your own advocate, for yourself or for your child. You should take this exhortation— Ask and ye shall receive—to every chapter in this book. Go step by step through the chapters as they are relevant to your circumstances, and do not be afraid to ask.

There is an old story about confronting your fears which may be useful to you on your journey to help your child. Visualize this: you are a zebra minding your own business while munching on some grass. It's the rainy season, so the brush and trees are thick with foliage.

Suddenly, a huge male lion steps out from the brush. You stop munching, frozen. You lock eyes with the lion. Then he opens his mouth and roars, and the ground shakes beneath your feet. Your bowels turn to liquid. Your muscles bunch, ready for flight. You can feel your body begin to turn one hundred and eighty degrees to run in the opposite direction.

STOP!! You are running the wrong way!

Remember this: RUN TO THE ROAR!

Are you rubbing your eyes? Wondering if you read this incorrectly? No. Because the female lions are the real hunters, and they are lying in wait for you as you run *from* the roar. That was their game plan in the first place. In reality, that huge lion is old, toothless, and maybe has arthritis in his hips. He couldn't chase you down if his life depended on it. No, his task is to scare you enough so you turn tail and run directly into the waiting deathtrap. So plan ahead, and don't do that. When you are confronted with the thing you fear the most, confront it directly. Face it down. Run to the roar. You will likely find out that this thing—a public speaking engagement, looking for a new job, going through the process of getting appropriate educational services for your child—cannot harm you. You are stronger and braver than it is. Even if your bowels turn to liquid from time to time.

But first you have to ask. So, what should you ask for? The answer to that question might be different for every person who reads this book, and may be different at various times of a reader's, and a child's, life.

In previous chapters, I have told you some of the 'who, what, where, and when' of making requests of your Child Study Team. If you have a big ask, such as referring your child to the Child Study Team and asking for a full evaluation, or asking for a significant change in your child's program, always put your request in writing. If your child is not classified, send your request directly to the Director of Special Services. If you have a case manager, send the request to the case manager, but make sure you copy the Director of Special Services by cc'ing him on your request.

It's okay to send such a request via email, but I would suggest you:

- Formalize it by writing a separate letter and attaching it to your cover email.

- Sign it with ink and scan it and send, or sign it electronically.

- Make sure you put a date on the letter.

I suggest keeping a separate email folder for all correspondence related to your child. It may get to the point when you need subfolders for ease of reference. However, in addition to keeping electronic files, ALWAYS keep a printed copy of this type of correspondence. Have you heard the joke about computers? There are two kinds: computers that have crashed, and computers that haven't crashed yet. So, print those documents and start a chronologic binder so you can stay organized and find things when you need them.

If you have a small ask, you could ask the staff directly. If, for instance, you are asking to meet with the teacher on a regular basis to share information and monitor your child's progress, you can ask the teacher directly. Many teachers are great about doing this. If the teacher is scattered or defensive or hostile, talk to your case manager about wanting to meet with the CM and the teacher to monitor your child's progress. Be prepared to support your request with valid reasons (i.e., "Carly is not keeping pace with her peers in reading fluency and comprehension. The teacher has begun a new instructional method and I'd like us to monitor it carefully."). Then follow up your verbal request with a memorializing email. For example:

Thank you for your cooperation in setting up regular meetings with me and (teacher's name) every first Thursday of the month to monitor Carly's reading fluency and comprehension. Would you please bring any classwork, tests, or quizzes that will help monitor her progress? Thank you so much.

I'd probably follow that up with a reminder email twenty-four to forty-eight hours in advance of the meeting. You could email the CM and the teacher and say you are looking forward to the meeting and you are just double-checking that you are meeting at X o'clock and would the CM please reply to both of you to confirm the location of the meeting. Remember to bring your binder, journal, or notebook, or whatever log you are using to keep details about how your child is doing at home and in the community. In the case of the struggling Carly, the parent might have notes about how her inability to read hinders her and humiliates her in real life. Maybe she can't even read which is the women's restroom in a restaurant. Maybe a younger sibling outpaces her at home and anywhere the family goes. Maybe she cannot read directions on a game she would like to play with her friends, so she contrives ways to get someone else to do it without revealing she cannot read. All of those details are important.

Remember that, if you do need to send a request to the Director of Special Services, it's always good form to speak to your CM first. You don't want her to feel sideswiped, and rules of hierarchy do apply. Make sure you are succinct and offer the best three reasons why you are making the request so that she can talk to the director herself in an intelligent and informed way. A case manager can sometimes be your best advocate. If she believes that your child needs a different kind of service or instruction, or even a different placement, she may be willing to go to bat for you.

Just don't count on it. Be careful whom you trust.

And put it in writing.

Remember the old Chinese proverb, "The shortest pencil is longer than the longest memory."

Parents routinely ask me whether they should send their requests by certified mail RRR, or Return Receipt Requested. This is not necessary and sends a signal that you are already a potentially litigious parent. Just keep copies of *what* you sent, whether via email or another carrier, and keep note of *when* you sent it. The law has its own safeguard called the Mailbox Rule. Under the law, once you post a letter, unless it is returned to you, that letter is *presumed by law to have reached its destination.*

You may wonder when you should ask for your child to be fully evaluated by the CST, or for changes to your child's program. The answer is as soon as possible. Children grow and change so quickly, and getting your child the *right* program, also known under the law as the "appropriate" program, will allow your child to reach her potential, to be happy in her school career, to make friends, to feel hope. Every child deserves this. But make sure you have support to make your requests and, if you have several requests for changes, it is better to make them all at once rather than coming back again and again.[21] If you do that, your CM may get tired of you and think you will never be satisfied. This is the last thing you ever want her to think when she sees you in the hallway or when she sees an email from you in her inbox. It will simply make your life, and your child's life, more difficult.

Another thing to keep in mind is that you should never ask for the "best" program, or say you want the "best" program. Remove that word from your special education vocabulary and replace it with "appropriate program" and a program that offers your child "significant learning" and "meaningful educational benefit." That program may include social skills, adaptive physical education, specialized therapies, testing modifications such as testing orally, testing with a familiar examiner, and testing in a small setting separate from the classroom. There are a myriad of modifications, accommodations, aids and services which school districts can, and do, provide to students with special needs. But your child's program should be developed specifically for your child's unique needs.

---

[21] Of course, your child's needs will change from year to year, and you should ask for changes as needed. But if you are in an evaluation sequence in a given year, gather up all the requests first and make them at one time.

There have been court cases in which judges compared a classified child's program to a car. The first judge reasoned that school districts are not responsible to provide a classified student with a "Cadillac" type of education, only a "serviceable Chevy." Another judge later returned to this automobile metaphor and added that school districts are responsible for providing programs with the "safety and security of a Volvo." Since the reference is metaphorical, what it actually means is open to interpretation. But you should know that this decision is out there and is still good law.

The United States Supreme Court decided a special education case in March 2017 to which we refer as *Endrew F.* [22] That is the child's first name and the first initial of his last name to maintain his privacy. This case was significant in that the Supreme Court of the United States of America does not typically decide special education cases. There was a split in the Federal District courts and the Supreme Court agreed to take on the challenge of deciding the appropriate standard which would then be effective nationwide.

In deciding this case, Chief Justice Roberts, writing for a unanimous court, observed that most children with disabilities are capable, with needed supports, of meeting grade level academic standards. The *Endrew* decision requires school districts to provide these students with special education designed to enable them to become academically proficient and to advance from grade to grade. For the small group of students with significant cognitive disabilities who cannot meet grade level standards, *Endrew* requires schools to provide special education that enables those children to meet challenging and

---

[22] *Endrew F. v. Douglas County Sch. Dist. RE-1*, 137 S. Ct. 988, 1000 (2017).

"appropriately ambitious" goals. For those students, progress may be measured against "alternate academic achievement standards" designed to promote further education, work, and independence.

Now you know what to ask for. But how do you do it? With what attitude? You don't have to go in gangbusters, pent up and ready for a battle. You may never have one. Remember the guy at the newspaper kiosk and do not let others dictate your behavior. It's very simple, really. In making any request, mind your manners. Be polite, be respectful. Remember Desiderata:

"...As far as possible, without surrender, be on good terms with all persons. Speak your truth quietly and clearly; ...Exercise caution in your business affairs, for the world is full of trickery. But let this not blind you to what virtue there is; many persons strive for high ideals, and everywhere life is full of heroism..."

The author, Max Ehrmann, might have been talking about your interactions with the Child Study Team. Most CST members choose their professional fields because they are compassionate people who want to help children. Even virtually all directors of special services were once CST members. They have many virtues, and may strive for high ideals in that profession, especially when they are young and idealistic. However, school districts are no different than many other businesses or job sites: there is a definite hierarchy with both official and unofficial agendas which may impact how people treat you and your requests.

For example, I once had a case in an affluent northern New Jersey town which involved an eleven-year-old girl who had a pretty significant reading disorder. The district had been a really solid school district for many years and the CST had made many attempts to institute programming designed to ameliorate this kid's reading disability. Despite everyone's hard work and the passage of a couple of years, this kid was falling further and further behind. To make matters worse, she had begun to despair, to cry and scream at night over her homework, which had become a nightly torture for the child and for her parents. The child lost hope and had begun to exhibit withdrawal from her friends and extracurricular activities. Her parents were at their wit's end.

We had private evaluations done and the recommendations came back to move this girl immediately to a private special-education school that specialized in reading disabilities. I made the request to the school district. Two unfortunate changes had recently occurred in the district which made our case much more difficult. Number one: the district had hired a new Director of Special Services, a real stuffed shirt who cared only about being right and lording his position over everyone. Number two: the district had just spent nine million dollars (yup, that was $9,000,000.00) on the acquisition of a very significant sports amenity. It must have been nice to get that contract.

It was the huge expenditure which made the district reluctant to send this struggling child out of district. The attitude of the stuffed shirt director was the final nail in the coffin of that request.

It was time to escalate the ask. I filed for due process.[23] We had mediation, which failed, then went to court for a settlement conference with a judge. Given the excellent data from the

---

[23] Chapter Eleven will explain due process.

professional expert reports, I was able to settle the case and the struggling student went on to attend an excellent specialized school nearby. Pretty soon, her parents were telling me they had "a new kid" on their hands. She jumped out of bed in the morning, got ready for school by herself, was ready to go twenty minutes early, came home bubbling over with joy and happiness that she was learning to read, and that she had friends who were just like her. I've said it before and I'll say it again: **Nothing succeeds like success.**

You may be thinking that all of this is an overreaction. Maybe you think that all lawyers are untrustworthy and out to make a buck. Maybe you really trust your CST and think that they are the professionals, so they are in the best position to make the decisions. Why, then, should you ask for anything other than what they offer you?

It's a great question and deserves thoughtful consideration. What do you do in other areas of your life? If you get a medical diagnosis and are told you need surgery, do you schedule it that day? Or do you get a second, and maybe a third, opinion? I would love to believe that school districts and the CSTs always do the right thing and are always accurate in their assessment. The extent to which that is not true, however, has kept my law firm in business, and growing, for more than forty years. Clients come to us; we don't have to go out and beat the bushes for them. Countless times I have listened to parents say, after hearing their rights at an initial consultation, "I wish I had never trusted the Child Study Team."

Therefore, remember to **trust your gut**. Don't ignore the sense that something is not right, that your child is not doing "fine" even though you get regular reassurances of same. It is your

89

child's future we are talking about. Only you are driving that train.

There are differences of opinion about how much to ask for. Some parents believe you should ask for every little thing under the sun and the school district needs to fund every dime. These parents can be pushy and nudgy and do not recognize how repulsive their behavior can be. Other parents are self-effacing and believe their child is lucky to get whatever services the district deigns to give them. School staff may both extremes of beliefs and behavior equally unappealing.

So, what's a parent to do? First, use the recommendations in the earlier chapters to figure out what your child needs. Then ask for all of it. Include items that are minor; you can easily let them go if you have to negotiate. In the end, since an IEP is a team effort, it is often a compromise.

Whenever you do ask for a meeting of any kind, but especially an IEP meeting, it is wise to send in advance anything you would like the team to discuss and consider as part of your child's program. That gives them time to review your data, your documents, your questions, your requests, or your expert reports. Ask the recipients (all of them) via email to confirm that they have received whatever you have sent. Politely ask them to review so you can all have meaningful discussion at the meeting.

CHAPTER NINE
Do Not Forsake the Very Good for the Perfect: What to Do When the CST Says 'No.'

Whenever the school district refuses your request for updated evaluations or a change in classification or programming, it's time to take stock and evaluate where you're at. One thing to keep in mind is this: Do not forsake the very good for the perfect.

What is the very good, you may ask? Assess the following factors:

- Have you gotten any changes to the program at all?

- If so, what percentage of your "ask" did the district agree to provide?

- Did you get all or most of your big-ticket items, the educational programming provisions that may mean the most to your child?

- Is your child likely to make progress in the program as agreed to or proposed by the district right now?

If so, consider stopping while you're ahead. If, in the cold light of day, you think this program may enable your child to make progress, my suggestion is to tell your case manager and the Child Study Team that, even though you believe your child needs the other elements of programming that they refused, you would like to trust their judgment at this time. You could tell them that at the meeting, or you could wait till later. It is advisable to give yourself time to retreat from any of these meetings, process what happened, and to think it through.

If you *are* going to wait, thank the Child Study Team and the other meeting participants and tell them you have a lot to consider. Later, if you have made your decision to go with the mostly-appropriate program, tell your case manager personally, either in person or via a phone call. Then—remember the Chinese pencil??—memorialize this decision in writing to each and every meeting participant. Why? You want everyone at that meeting to hear that you trust them, that you appreciate their work, and that you are a reasonable person. This does not mean that you actually do trust them. Remember *act as if?* Here, you can act as if you trust them. You don't need to really trust them, or you can trust them for the moment. Think of it any way you prefer. But make sure to keep notes about the meeting. Include what you asked for, why you asked for it, who refused you and why. Keep these notes with all of your other notes and documents in chronological order in your binder. Remember to include the email in which you concede your position to their professional judgment. **This is a critical part of your paper trail.** Remember that, if this program is not as successful as the CST has promised, you now have tangible and salient evidence which demonstrates how reasonable you have been and how the district has failed to provide your child with a program that ensures he make "meaningful educational progress."

But I'm feeling discouraged and ill-used.

It's important to remember at this time, when you may feel discouraged, that *you* have made the school district engage in this federally- and state-mandated process which guarantees certain rights to you and your child. Perhaps the CST did not want to give any of those modifications, accommodations, or instructional strategies to your child. It was through your parenting, your observation, your determination to ensure your child's current and future success that you got as far as you did. It is very important to recognize this and to celebrate the victories along the way.

If you are like some of my clients, you may not want to wait to see if your child makes progress. You want to go in now, hit them with the big artillery, the big guns, a big stick, for heaven's sake. Why wait?

Why wait, indeed. It was actually those two words that caused me to go to law school when I did even though I had a perfectly good career as a Child Study Team member and psychotherapist. I had become quite restless as I saw and heard other staff complaining about how much work they had to do and how they could never get it done during the allotted hours of the work day. I also noticed that those same complainers engaged in a lot of wasted time and gossip. Somehow this alleged lack of time did not affect me, probably since I did not hang around and gossip with them.

It did leave me feeling as if I did not belong in this group, however, and I began to explore my options for a doctoral degree. It didn't take long for me to focus in on the law. That way, I reasoned, I could assist many more students to be successful than I had on my school caseload. I talked with my husband until I had chewed his ear off. One winter evening, we sat in our car in a favorite spot discussing the matter. I said I thought I should wait to go to law school until all the kids were grown. He replied, "Why wait?" The proverbial famous last words. So, I took my LSAT's, went off to law school (with a husband and three teenagers in the house), and here I am, decades later. Why wait, indeed.

There really are some good reasons for waiting. It all depends on an overall assessment of the facts. If your child is making progress in her program, it may be better to wait and monitor. While waiting, continue to make your paper trail and to build your evidence. Lawyers talk about building their case one brick of evidence at a time. Each brick is important, but it takes a lot of bricks to make a wall. Be patient. This is a marathon, not a sprint.

Have I Wasted Those Expert Evaluations?

If you *are* waiting, you may be wondering if you have wasted money on those expert evaluations. In my experience, good expert evaluations are invaluable. Good evaluations:

- Provide a baseline of data demonstrating exactly where your child is functioning at the moment of assessment

- Determine and mark your child's aptitude

- Determine and mark your child's achievement

- Make recommendations for programming

- Provide the parents with important information about how their child learns, which parents can utilize at home and in the community

- Provide the parents with important information about how their child learns, which parents can share with teachers

- Support the findings with a reasonable scientific certainty, the standard required in a court of law.

Furthermore, in the next year or two, should you need proof that your child is not progressing as expected, you can have the same expert(s) do discrete updates of the previous testing. The same expert would compare the updated testing which had used the same testing instruments to the earlier findings and conclusions. It would then be clear whether or not your child is making progress.

Can I get my money back?

You may want to know whether you can have your school district pay for your expert evaluations. The answer is, once again, that depends. The law allows parents to ask their school district to provide private independent evaluations under certain circumstances. See Chapter 2. Once you have retained an expert and paid for the evaluation yourself, however, the likelihood that the school district will agree to reimburse you is small to non-existent. If you have a great relationship with your school district, anything is possible, but don't get your hopes up, especially if you find yourself in an adversarial role with the district. While the school staff, especially the CST, are professionals and should not take it

95

personally when a parent disagrees with them, the reality is, they do. I have had some cases in which I was able to get reimbursement of these costs, usually partial reimbursement, as one of the terms of a larger, comprehensive settlement agreement.

By the way, people like to tell tall tales, and I have heard some doozies about what other parents and attorneys were able to get in settlement agreements. I have been shocked at the things people brag about, especially in affluent, competitive school districts. Word to the wise: Don't believe everything you hear, and don't make yourself feel bad by comparing what you got from your school district with what someone else tells you they got. Unless you see it in writing and signed by a judge in an official document, it's likely that it didn't happen.

Medical insurance will sometimes pick up all or part of the cost of private evaluations. When you make the initial contact with the expert, make sure to tell her that you would like to submit the invoice to your insurance company for reimbursement. That way, the expert will know you need an appropriate invoice.

I'm too angry to let it go.

"Those dastardly dirty-dealing double-crossers shouldn't get away with this!!"

When it comes to incompetent and dishonest school staff, and to students with disabilities, I am right there with you. Nothing makes my blood boil more than finding out that someone has taken advantage of a kid with a disability. That is a population which is twice-vulnerable. They are young and innocent, and they have some type of challenge which makes them that much more susceptible. If you are too angry and upset to simply forgive and forget, that's understandable. But stop right here and ask yourself, "What best serves my child?"

It's okay to be angry when someone neglects or hurts your child. If that anger drives you to take action to heal the neglect or injury, then ride that wave. But you're the parent. You have to put your own pride, stubbornness, vanity, or hurt aside to keep your eyes on the goal: the right programming for your child in order to reach the ultimate reward of success, and meaningful growth year after year, so your child can be catapulted into appropriate post-secondary education, rewarding employment, and as much independence as he is capable of.

But how do you do that? How do you not seethe with anger every time you see these people in school, every time you get an inane email from the teacher saying Henry did fine in school today?

Find your feet. Take two deep breaths. (I'm really not kidding and this really does help). Now go back to Chapter Six and review—and practice—the techniques I laid out there.

One other thing you might do is to join the district Special Education Parents Advisory Council or SEPAC. Both federal and state law mandate that every school district must establish a SEPAC. A SEPAC is designed to be a self-governing body and is open to all parents of children with special needs and to other interested parties. It is a public body which should advise the local school committee on matters relating to the education of and safety of students with disabilities. The SEPAC must meet regularly with school officials to participate in the planning, development, and evaluation of your district's special education programs. Through the SEPAC, you can find other like-minded parents who face the same challenges you are facing. They can offer support, good advice, and the benefit of their experience. One word of warning, however. In my experience, school districts often have their hands in the SEPAC and try to oversee, monitor, and even stifle the free-flow of information amongst the parents and the speakers whom they might bring in from time to time. The best course of action is to attend the SEPAC meetings and find out if there are any related groups which are private and which exclude school district staff. Meet with that group or create one, but stay involved with the SEPAC, too. The SEPAC can help make needed changes in district policy and procedures.

I don't trust the Child Study Team any more. How can I make sure they implement the IEP?

Good question. During my thirty years as a psychotherapist, Child Study Team member, and lawyer representing parents of students with special needs, I have encountered a legion of parents who have lost trust in the teachers, the case manager, the Child Study Team, the Director of Special Services, and sometimes even the entire school district. It's like that old nursery rhyme, For Want of a Horseshoe Nail. Remember how it goes?

For Want of a Horseshoe Nail

For want of a nail the shoe was lost.
For want of the shoe the horse was lost.
For want of the horse the rider was lost.
For want of the rider the message was lost.
For want of the message the battle was lost.
For want of the battle the kingdom was lost.
And all for the want of a horseshoe nail.

Your "nail" could be the misstep of any one of these people, which could result in your child's program collapsing like a house of cards. So, what's a parent to do?

Plenty, that's what. Remember all the tools I have given you in the previous chapters. Although some of those tools are simple, I still use them because they still work. You still use a hammer, a screwdriver, a kitchen spatula, and a toothbrush, right? In fact, what would you do without those simple, basic tools? This situation is no different, so do not allow yourself to feel overwhelmed, outgunned, hoodwinked, or unable. You *can* do this. You *will* do this. You *must* do this. This is your child's life we are talking about. Who better to do this job than the person who has brought this child into the world and nurtured that child to this point? So, chin up. Find your feet. Take two deep slow breaths. Activate that vagus nerve. Remember, there is no sabretooth tiger. Run to the roar to reclaim your child's life.

The "roar" here is your inability to be in school every minute of every day to see what the teachers, the paraprofessional aides, the case manager, and the related service therapists see. How, then, can you discover and find out whether the school district is implementing your child's IEP with integrity? How also can you monitor your child's progress or regression?

- One way is to use the IEP as the tool it was meant to be. Look at the PLAAFP. This delineates your child's functioning at the time he was tested, as noted, or when the IEP was written. Create a chart and compare your child's progress over time as reflected in her classwork, quizzes, test scores, your own personal observation, and that of any other significant person in your child's life (i.e., karate teacher, boy scout leader). Keep your charts in your organizational binder.

- Another example is to keep a flow chart of your child's goals and objectives and keep track of how classwork, quizzes, and test scores support progress or regression. Keep your charts in your organizational binder.

- Another way to monitor the implementation is to develop a chart of all services, accommodations, modifications, specialized instruction, for example, that the IEP provides. Then seek feedback from those persons with whom you have cultivated relationships per Chapter 6 and elicit feedback. Keep track of that feedback in your chart. Keep your charts in your organizational binder.

- You could also develop a checklist which notes the most important things that should occur during your child's day. Ask your teacher if she will fill it out on a daily basis. You can even ask the CM to include the checklist in the

IEP as a form of monitoring your child's progress. Keep these checklists in your organizational binder.

- A final, and very effective way, is to have your expert(s) go into school and observe your child. You will need to arrange this with the case manager, but the district does not have the right to refuse you access to observe your child's progress. That right extends to any expert you retain. Here are some of the particulars of that right:

- The Board of Education in <u>S.B. and K.B. o/b/o P.B. v. Park Ridge BOE</u>, a New Jersey case, acknowledged that a parent must be given the opportunity to observe the proposed educational placement prior to implementation of the IEP in accordance with <u>N.J.A.C. 6A:14-4.1(k)</u>. <u>OAL DKT. No. EDS 13813-08</u>. However, it argued, that provision did not apply to an outside consultant.

- In the <u>Park Ridge</u> case, Judge Richard McGill responded by citing the difficulties with the district's argument: "First," he wrote, "remedial social legislation is to be liberally construed to achieve its beneficent purposes. <u>Squeo v. Comfort Control Corp.</u>, 99 <u>N.J.</u> 588, 596 (1985). As such, IDEA should be read broadly to achieve its purposes. In this context, the parent needs the assistance of an expert to present a case. It would follow that the term 'parent' should be read to authorize the parents' expert to observe the proposed program." <u>Id.</u> at 8. Neither parents themselves, nor their experts, may be denied the observation, materials and information necessary to evaluate a program. <u>Id.</u> at

10. In order to evaluate a program, an expert must have facts and data concerning the program, as well as observation of and interviews with the personnel, including teachers, aides and therapists." Id. at 12-13. The observation must be of sufficient duration for the expert to develop her opinion. Id. at 13. Judge McGill found the District's attempts at restricting the expert's time unreasonable. Id. at 13-14.

- In a document from the federal Office of Special Education Programs ("OSEP"),[24] OSEP upheld a parent's right to go into her child's school to observe and to have her expert observe as well.

- In a subsequent case, School Board of Manatee County v. L.H. ex rel. D.H.,[25] the administrative law judge agreed. The court rejected the school district's argument that Letter to Mamas applied only to IEEs at the public's expense. This solidified the parent's legal right to have their own independent expert(s) observe their child in his local public school district program and to render an independent opinion. When parents seek to arrange their expert's observation, school districts should refrain from adversarial behavior toward that parent and should treat them as if there were no potential dispute.

- These cases demonstrate that parents have the right to observe in order to effectively exercise their right to an

---

[24] Letter to Mamas, dated May 26, 2004 (42 IDELR 10)
[25] No. 8:08-cv-1435-T-33MAP, 2009 WL 3231914 (M.D. Fla. Sept. 30, 2009) Manatee County, 2009 WL 3231914, at *3.

independent evaluation, the right to information about or participation in the IEP, or most significantly, the right to present meaningful well-founded testimony at a hearing.

However, getting your expert in to observe can be a tricky balance because the school district does have the right and the obligation to run the school safely and effectively. The principal or Director of Special Services can limit the frequency and duration of expert observations. An ideal observation would be a full-day visit so the expert can observe the student getting on the bus at home, disembarking at school, and throughout the student's entire day until she is dropped off at home at the end of the school day. These days, such a long observation is rare. School districts will usually not allow it. You may have to bargain and negotiate with the case manager or directly with the Director of Special Services to obtain as much time as possible. Two hours has become standard.

If you must bargain for the amount of time your expert needs, you can try having an in-person discussion with the director. Typically, though, you will be required to use your CM as a middleman. Impress upon the CM the need for her to share the following information with the director:

- Your desire to be an active part of the IEP team

- Your desire to have an objective pair of eyes observe your child

- The skill and experience of your expert

- The need for the expert to see as much of your child's functioning as possible across domains (structured time, including a variety of classroom instruction; managing transitions from bus to building and from class to class; unstructured time during lunch or recess).

Remember to memorialize this in writing to the case manager and to the director. This is part of your paper trial. Keep the letter (I suggest a letter; it's more formal that way, but it is okay to send the letter via a cover email) in your organizational binder. Remember: if it isn't in writing, it didn't happen. The shortest pencil is longer than the longest memory.

CHAPTER TEN
Application of Your Knowledge and Therapeutic Techniques.

One of my clients, whom I'll call Laura Simpson[26], was the mother of an 11-year-old girl with a reading disorder. Laura's daughter was falling behind in the school district's program. After expert evaluations, we requested the district place the daughter at a specialized private school. The district refused.

After I filed for due process, the district indicated it was interested in mediating the dispute. Laura asked me if she could present at mediation. While I normally would not want a parent to do the talking at the mediation table, Laura was an intelligent and personable woman who had a pretty steady demeanor. For those reasons, I took a risk and worked with her on a number of techniques which I have related in this book. I presented the initial legal basis for the request for a change in program and placement. Then Laura spoke. As I sat next to her at the conference table and listened to her presentation to the school officials, I marveled at her composure and the emotional pull of her words. What really made it powerful is that Laura had scrubbed out any trace of resentment and anger she had toward the district staff. She did not criticize the staff or the work they had done with her daughter. She made the presentation about her daughter and her daughter's needs. She was kind and she

---

[26] All names and characteristics have been changed to protect client confidentiality.

made sure to praise whatever she could about the district while highlighting her daughter's special needs.

When she was done speaking, the district staff picked up their things and left the room to go and caucus privately. After the door shut behind them, Laura turned to me and sagged. It had taken a huge effort for her to keep it together. But she did it, using many of the effective therapeutic strategies in this book.

About ten minutes later, the school district staff returned to the room to deliver their decision: they had decided to agree to send Laura's daughter to the out-of-district private school. All of the expert evaluations, legal knowledge, relationship-building, and therapeutic techniques had paid off in a big way for Laura's daughter. The district placed her in the private school where she learned to read, made friends like her, felt as if she belonged, and became a happy and successful student. Laura had "a new kid" on her hands. **Nothing succeeds like success**.

Laura had me for a guide through this process, and her case was successful. You also have me for a guide through the knowledge and techniques in this book. She achieved her goals for her child, and you can, too.

Here are some of the therapeutic techniques which I and my clients have used successfully in getting the right programs for students. If you take the time to learn and practice these techniques, you, too, will be able to develop better relationships, smoother communication with others, and the ability to manage and modulate your own emotions, leading to less stress and more joy and happiness in your life.

The first technique you will learn in this chapter is the Therapeutic Alliance.

A therapeutic alliance technically refers to the relationship between a healthcare professional and a client. It is the relationship within which they relate to one another to effect positive change in the client and the client's life. It is also called a working alliance.

Technicalities aside, you can utilize a working alliance with important members of your child's educational team. But first you need to know the steps to create such an alliance.

On its website, www.goodtherapy.org lists ways in which therapists can strengthen alliances with their patients. Here is that list extrapolated to fit your needs vis a vis your child's educational team:

1. **Help the teacher, aide, or case manager feel more welcome in your company.** This is a little harder when you are in their territory, but not impossible. For instance, if you were hosting a meeting with the teacher in your home or office, you could ensure the temperature was pleasant, put on soothing music, make sure the lighting was good and the seating was comfortable. When visiting the teacher or case manager, you can try to visit or meet when that staff member has enough time and is not distracted by other responsibilities. You can let her know in advance the reason you want to meet, if it's a formal meeting. That way, she won't be wondering or concerned about it. Make sure you are clear about your expectations, and don't skimp on praise and positive feedback. If you are just dropping by—and that is a good idea sometimes, you never know what you'll find—

you can be sensitive about whether it is a good time or not. And you could always bring a cup of her favorite coffee.

2. **Know that relationships take time.** It will take time to build relationships with the school staff who work closely with your child. Follow the recommendations in Chapter 6 and allow the relationships to unfold.

3. **Never criticize the staff.** Your child's teachers, aides, case managers, and other staff will make mistakes. They will, at times, cut corners, be rushed, miss important signals. They may be abrupt, curt or even rude to you. Remember the man buying the newspaper from the rude sales agent and do not allow the staff's behavior to dictate your own.

This does not mean that you should overlook incompetence or refusal to implement your child's IEP or other appropriate educational steps. You should definitely note this with specificity in the notes in your organizational binder. But try and look at it from the staff member's point of view. Was it as bad as it appeared? Could there have been another motivation that you missed at first? Are you the one with blinders on? If possible, talk over the situation with the other parent or a trusted confidant.

If the staff person did make a misstep which you must correct, ask to meet with that staff at the end of the school day, if possible. Bring up the circumstances in a non-judgmental way and explain that is what you noticed or experienced. Ask the teacher or staff if they have a different point of view. See if you can agree on what happened and how it might be rectified or done differently in the future. These types of discussions, if managed correctly, can contribute greatly to the strength of your relationship with your child's educators. Most likely, they will appreciate your understanding and low-key approach. After the meeting, write a summary of what occurred for your organizational binder.

4. **Manage your own emotions.** It takes time to learn how to recognize your own emotions, and it takes practice to set them aside or utilize them to achieve your goals. The techniques and suggestions in this book, especially in Chapter 6, can help you do that, but you will need to practice. It doesn't take much time and it actually will make you feel happier, calmer, and more in control of your life.

5. **Talk with the educator about what she wants from the school year for her students.** This is an amazing and potentially fulfilling way to earn the trust and respect of your child's educators. It may even have a beneficial effect on their performance. Think about it. Think about a time when someone paid attention to you and to your goals and aspirations in life. These days, it's unusual for anyone to spend much time getting to know one another. We are all subject to constant electronic distractions from our jobs, our families, and our community obligations. Given the opportunity for an educator to discuss what motivated her to go into this field may help rekindle her downtrodden hopes and dreams. Do not underestimate the power of you.

6. **Ask more or different questions.** Some people are reticent to discuss their hopes and dreams, especially with a relative

stranger. But if you ask open-ended questions[27] that show you are curious and really interested in the answers, the educator may open up to you. Don't rush it. Really listen to the answers. Ask follow-up questions that demonstrate you heard what she is saying.

7. **Focus on the teacher or case manager's needs**. You don't need to do this often. After all, the school staff is there to do a professional job for which they are paid. Nevertheless, you have an agenda and it is well worth your while to befriend and support those who teach and case manage your child. The returns will be well worth any investment you make. Therefore, make it a point to learn about anything the teacher or case manager needs from you, from the other class parents, or from any Parent-Teacher Organization which exists within your district. If you can help meet that need, do it.

The second technique is Voice Modulation. This simple technique will help you control or adjust your voice. The idea is to use your voice and tone to be a more effective communicator. It's pretty simple when you think about it and practice some basic rules.

1. **Slow down**. Most people who present publicly speak too fast, even if it's only to a small audience like an IEP team. It's usually because they are nervous. Recognize that the listeners need a little time to hear and digest what

---

[27] Open-ended questions are questions which cannot be answered with a one-word answer such as "No," "Yes," or "Maybe."

you are saying. Remember that what you are saying is important and needs to be heard. Pace yourself.

2. **Add pauses and emphasis in the right places.** Remember you are telling a story. Practice inserting a pause in different places, especially after you introduce yourself and when you want to let a point sink home.

3. **Speak clearly with a volume appropriate to the size of the audience and the space.** If you are in a small office with two other people, you can speak at normal conversational volume. If you are in a large conference room with fifteen people, you may have to project your voice so the person farthest away can hear you clearly.

4. **Vary your tone and inflection.** You don't want to speak in a monotone or the listeners will zone out.

5. **Do not umm and ah.** It is so easy to use these noises as fillers. Practice weeding them out. You will be a much more interesting and polished speaker if you do. However, don't beat yourself up if you slip up. Almost everyone umms once in a while.

6. **Believe your own story.** Pump yourself up before you start. Tell yourself, "I am making a difference in my child's life," and "I will be successful. Because I have the courage to do this, my child will be successful also." This will give you confidence.

7. **Practice.** Walk around your home and practice what you want to say. Once you've got that down, practice in front of a mirror or have a family member or trusted

friend sit and listen and give you constructive feedback when you're done.

The third technique is Visualization. Visualization is when you create images in your mind to enable yourself to find peace, alleviate stress, and achieve goals. Just as the body can experience a negative incident simply by thinking about it (one extreme example is posttraumatic stress disorder in which the person continues to re-experience a past trauma), you can train yourself to visualize positive life events and circumstances. The key is to focus on what you really want.

One form of this visualization is called WOOP. Based on twenty years of scientific research, WOOP has been proven effective in helping people achieve their goals. WOOPers have been successful in problem-solving, improving time management, losing weight, drinking less alcohol, improved school attendance and achievement. Go to www.woopmylife.org for more information and to practice the technique.

YouTube has numerous videos on visualization which you can access and learn. Try the following:

https://www.youtube.com/watch?v=YFImv3izCzE#:~:text=5%20Powerful%20visualisation%20techniques%20Think%20about%20this%3A%20everything,human%20creation%20exists%20first%20in%20our...%20Skip%20navigation

https://www.youtube.com/watch?v=3ECTX18pBDM

Don't stop until you find one that works for you.

The fourth technique is Mindfulness to Block Negative Emotions, including Emotional Contagion.

Negative emotions, like fear and anxiety, have helped our species survive for centuries. They trigger the fight or flight response in our primitive brain.

Professor Jud Brewer, MD, PhD, a psychiatrist, neuroscientist and associate professor at Brown University, described in the Harvard Business Review how anxiety, fear, and dread had spread through his class of undergraduate and graduate students in March 2020. The students were awaiting news about the university's decision to close in the face of the SARS-CoV2 (covid-19) pandemic.

Fear triggers the fight or flight response, yet these days there is no sabretooth tiger from which we must run to survive. Instead, as with Professor Brewer's students, the threat and even the response was uncertain, resulting in a growing anxiety.

Widespread use of social media contributes to the spread of emotional contagion. Professor Brewer noted, "Constant scrolling through the latest news on your phone or desktop is like walking by people who are sneezing fear. The more you read, the more you are likely to take on their worry, and spread it. The problem is that these emotions keep us from being able to think straight, and when overdone, they no longer protect us from dangers. Rather, they become the danger."

For you, as a parent of a child with special needs, the threat of emotional contagion can come from a number of sources. It could be internal, as a result of a difficult diagnosis.

Consider Arthur,[28] the child of one of my clients, who was diagnosed with severe autism. Although Arthur had severe challenges, he was functional and worked his programs well, making him quite independent. The family was happy.

Early one morning, the mother went to wake Arthur and found him in bed with a bloody mouth. Unable to find the source of the bleeding and concerned about his reaction to a trip to the emergency room, she took him to the pediatrician. A few days later, the news came back: Arthur had leukemia. Can you imagine the family's devastation? This was a threat to his health and life, and to the family's safety and security.

Arthur's mom was in a panic and called me. As I sat with her on the phone, I had her use the "Find Your Feet" technique. When we were finished, I taught her a technique I learned from Dr. Richard Nongard, a renowned hypnotist and clinician, called "3-2-1 Reset." I want you to try this right now as you are reading.

First, count your next three breaths. You do not need to alter your breathing. Simply be aware of the next three breaths. This tells your vagus nerve that you are not being threatened and that it can calm down.

Next, pick up your two hands to about shoulder height, palms facing forward. Now cross your arms and put each hand on the opposite shoulder. Give yourself a little squeeze. That gesture releases oxytocin, a hormone secreted by the posterior lobe of the pituitary gland. Often called the "love hormone," oxytocin

---

[28] All names and circumstances have been changed to protect client confidentiality.

promotes feelings of social bonding, well-being and love. Scientists and researchers are testing it as an anti-anxiety drug. By using this technique, you are giving yourself a little dose.

Finally, keep your hands on your shoulders for one minute as you breathe slowly. Try and keep your mind empty. Focus on your breath.

Then check in. Has your heart rate slowed? Is your breathing deeper and more regular?

Practice using this technique and watch as you discover a new and simple way to alleviate panic.

This technique worked for Arthur and it will work for you, too. All you need to do is do it!

The other good news is that Arthur's leukemia was a non-lethal variety. He was treated and recovered, and the family continued their happy, imperfect journey through life.

<u>The fifth technique is Fogging.</u> Fogging is a useful communication technique when others are being demanding or manipulative. Rather than being put into a defensive posture, fogging allows you to remain calm without acquiescing to outrageous or obnoxious demands.

How it works: when someone confronts you in an angry way, you can respond calmly by agreeing with anything they say that is actually true. By remaining calm and non-argumentative, the other person will usually stop being aggressive.

Here's an example: You have recently filed for mediation (see Chapter 11) and are dropping off your second-grader's lunch in the main office. You run into the case manager in the hallway and she is fit to be tied. Looking quite harried, she starts in on you:

Case Manager: "Well, Mrs. Brown, I just found out you filed for mediation. You could have told me first."

You: "Yes, it's true I filed for mediation."

Case Manager: "The director just ripped me a new one about it."

You: "Ah, yes, filing for mediation is bound to cause some upset."

Case Manager: "Upset! This is beyond upset. Why in the world didn't you speak to me first?"

You: "It's natural to feel upset. We feel upset, too. But that's what mediation is for, to help us work through it."

You get the idea. Don't get pulled into the other person's upset and aggression. Picture yourself as a large, gray wall of thick fog into which the other person is throwing barbs. They just disappear into the fog because you are being pleasant and not returning the barbs.

The sixth technique is the Stuck Record. This is a great one and so easy to do with a little practice. You just simply repeat what you want without allowing yourself to be provoked into anger or upset. In the incident of the attack by the case manager above, it would go like this:

Case Manager: "Well, Mrs. Brown, I just found out you filed for mediation. You could have told me first."

You: "Yes, it's true I filed for mediation."

Case Manager: "The director just ripped me a new one about it."

You could remain quiet here as this doesn't really require a response. Try and wait patiently with a slight smile on your face to see what she'll say next. It probably won't take long for your silence to provoke another comment. Most people are quite uncomfortable with silence and will try and fill it.

Case Manager: "Why in the world didn't you speak to me first?"

You: "I actually did speak to you about it. Why don't you have a look at the mediation request and we can talk about it with the mediator."

Case Manager: "I don't remember you speaking to me about it."

You: "Why don't you review the mediation request and then we'll discuss it with the mediator."

This is a great technique for getting out of sticky situations without having to defend your actions. It can help you feel much calmer in what would otherwise have been a very upsetting situation.

The seventh technique is "Getting to Yes." It is based on the idea that, when you negotiate, you should focus not on your position vs. the district's position, but instead should focus on the interests of both sides and find a mutually-acceptable way to compromise. The authors of the wildly popular book by the same name, Getting to Yes, Roger Fisher, William Ury and Bruce Patton, focus on four steps in what they call "principled negotiation":

1. **Separate the people from the problem**. If you have already built relationships with district staff you are ahead of the game here. Do not focus on who did what here. Instead, focus on what you and the others are trying to accomplish. Most likely, that is to help your child make meaningful educational progress. Ask the district to look at the problem of how to satisfy both your and their interests.

2. **Focus on interests, not positions**. Don't assume you know what the school district's interests are. It might be money. It might be administrative convenience. But it may also be how to ensure that your child's program is appropriate. Talk about your interests. Listen when they talk about theirs. Then talk about what solution or options can satisfy both interests.

3. **Invent options for mutual gain**. This is where you and the district staff think outside the box. Sit and brainstorm together about what might work. Don't judge the ideas. Just get them down on paper. Think of how both sides will gain. Put yourself in the district's shoes and make sure you ask them to do the same.

4. **Insist on using objective criteria**. Using objective criteria helps take the wind out of the sails of battle. This is not a fight to the death. Everyone should think of objective criteria which can be used to come to resolution. I talk about some of that criteria in Chapter Nine.

The eighth technique is Kind Persistence. What's in a name? This technique. Kind Persistence is a mental stance which translates to facial expression, tone of voice, body posture, all culminating in a standing request for change. It is not arrogant, obnoxious, or aggressive. It is similar to the Stuck Record technique except you will be the initiator. You will make the request for change.

The ninth technique is Emotional Freedom Tapping or EFT. EFT is for you. It is a way to deal with negative emotions or physical pain when they threaten to overtake you, drag you down, or get in the way of you achieving your goals. It operates on the principles and physiology of acupressure. Instead of trying to learn by reading about it, go online and watch a video. I like Robin Bilazarian, a clinician and international EFT trainer. You can find one of her EFT videos at:

https://www.bing.com/videos/search?q=youtube+emotional +freedom+techniques+%26+tapping+instruction&docid=608 024668823751652&mid=ABCD22D965E488A3DA4EABCD 22D965E488A3DA4E&view=detail&FORM=VIRE

The tenth technique is Advocacy. Advocacy is not really a technique, but I include it here so that you are mindful that, when you are employing all of the knowledge and therapeutic techniques in this book, you are advocating.

Advocacy is any action that argues in favor of a cause or supports, defends or pleads on behalf of others.[29] Advocacy can be complicated and is comprised of many activities. There are three types of advocacy: Self-advocacy, Individual Advocacy, and Systems Advocacy. For your purposes, "advocacy" is all of

---

[29] Alliance for Justice website at www.mffh.org ; West Virginia University Center of Excellence in Disabilities.

the actions you have taken and will take in order to ensure your child's legal rights are met, including the rights to:

- An appropriate education

- Meaningful educational benefit

- Significant learning

- An appropriately ambitious IEP gauged to your child's ability, and

- Preparation for whatever post-secondary education, employment, and level of independence is appropriate for your child when she reaches the age of majority.

Self-Advocacy: Should I teach my child these techniques?

At some point, you will teach your child some or all of these techniques. That should be done according to your child's intellectual and emotional abilities and his development stage.

Bringing a friend or family member to an IEP Meeting

My recommendation is never to attend an IEP meeting alone if you can help it. If both parents are able to attend, that is the most beneficial so long as neither parent is so angry at the staff that the anger will act as an obstacle. Parents or guardians are permitted to bring anyone they want to their child's IEP meeting. If both parents cannot attend, then a capable grandparent, aunt, uncle or trusted friend is a good substitute. *Fair warning: if one of these people is an attorney, please have them leave the lawyer hat outside the door.* While attorney relatives and friends want to be helpful, they are trained in certain techniques that, unless they fully understand this area of the law, can backfire on you and put the district in a defensive mode. This will poorly serve your child and the flow of information from the district which you enjoyed before the meeting will dry up.

Recording a Meeting

Parents often ask me if they "should" record a meeting. As an attorney and advocate for children with disabilities, it has been my longstanding recommendation that parents should not record meetings. These days especially, when the rate of litigation against school districts has increased exponentially, plopping your electronic device on the conference table has a chilling effect on communication. That is exactly the *opposite* of what you want in a meeting with your school staff. You want to find out as much as you can about how your child is doing, and you want staffers to feel comfortable expressing their opinions and even admitting when things have not gone as they had hoped. This is less likely to happen if you record the meeting.

That said, some of my clients have recorded some amazing things which staff have revealed in meetings. Did it help us get an appropriate program for the child? Usually not. A parent's notes are almost as good, so make sure you take good notes, both during and after a meeting. And have your family member or trusted friend take notes, too. Put these directly in your organizational binder.

If you do decide to record a meeting, you will need to give the district advance written notice. Please be clear: you are not permitted to surreptitiously record meetings. If you ignore that rule, you will not be permitted to use that recording as evidence in any legal proceeding.

CHAPTER ELEVEN
If You Have Gotten This Far Without Relief, It's Time to Take Out the Big Guns.

There may come a time when you have a dispute with your school district. You have been diligent, patient and polite. You have overlooked some mistakes, avoidable delays, even some rudeness. You have taken the high road. Turned the other cheek, even. But you have gotten nowhere. You have done everything correctly. You have checked out your hunches by carefully monitoring your child's progress. You may have even obtained expert evaluations. You went to the IEP meeting with an open mind because you wanted to hear the CST and other staff's thoughts about what you had so diligently researched and discovered. Sadly, at the meeting, you were met by a wall of stony expressions. The air was frigid with disapproval. You were miserable and confused at the meeting. *I thought I was part of this team*, you may have thought while you struggled to process the underlying emotions and messages from all the participants while discussing your data and your requests.

The answer is, you *are* part of the team! Parents are as much a part of the IEP team as the case manager, the teacher, or the Child Study Team member. The law says so. It is not uncommon, however, for the school district staff to treat the parents as if they are know-nothings.

First of all, relax. Disputes are a common occurrence in the course of human events. Think about how often you argued with your siblings growing up, or how often you argue with your spouse. We expect to have disagreements. Sometimes we can agree to disagree. Sometimes not.

Once you have made a request for change in evaluations, classification, or programming and your school district[30] refuses despite all of your hard work, cooperation, and hard evidence, you now have a dispute. Okay, now what?

At this point, there is no going back. You have discovered what your child needs. The school district has refused to provide it. Now you have to go and get it.

File for Mediation and Due Process.

Mediation and Due Process are the mechanisms in place to resolve disputes regarding evaluation, classification, programming, and placement. To file, go onto your state's Department of Education website and search for Mediation and Due Process Form or Dispute Resolution Form. If you cannot locate it, call your state Department of Education or contact your local library. Reference librarians are amazing repositories of information and should be able to help. Make sure you request both Mediation and Due Process. You will have more leverage that way as it tells the school district up front that you are willing to go farther should they not settle with you at Mediation. You will also be protecting yourself by maintaining

---

[30] Your local school district in which you live and where your child attends school is referred to in the law as your Local Educational Agency or LEA.

your child's program after Mediation ends if the school district is trying to remove programming.[31]

Download the form and fill it out, making sure to enter your name, your child's name, your contact information, your school district, the name of the school in which your child is enrolled, a description of the dispute you have with the school district, and the way in which you would like to see it resolved. You may want to attach a typed word document describing the dispute to the form itself. You want to make sure to include all the specifics of the dispute. Stick to the facts and be as succinct as possible. The DOE receives thousands of these forms every year. It is best to make their job as easy as possible. Therefore, write sentences that are clear and to the point. Do not say how you feel about what happened. Do not complain about the district's behavior. Stick to the facts about what your child needs, the facts which support the request you made, the interventions that were undertaken, what did not work, and the outcome you would like to see.

When you have included all the information, file it with the state Department of Education as indicated in your state. Make sure you send a copy to your school district Director of Special Services, and make sure to keep a copy for your records. Put it in your organizational binder.

The DOE will send you a notice that it has received your request and will contact you again to schedule Mediation. In the

---

[31] This is called Stay Put. It is a legal mechanism which arises automatically upon the filing of Mediation and/or Due Process and remains in place until the dispute is resolved.

meantime, your school district may contact you to schedule a Resolution Session.

Resolution Session or Mediation?

A Resolution Session may sound nicer and feel a little more comfortable than Mediation with a state-appointed mediator. However, in my experience, a Resolution Session is a complete waste of time and will only delay an appropriate outcome for your child.

Think about it. It's the same people who were together for an IEP meeting, in the same room, working on the same issue. Expecting a different outcome is the definition of insanity.[32] Kindly decline the offer of a Resolution Session and head straight for Mediation. At this point, strongly consider seeking the assistance of an attorney. If you have an attorney, that person will file for Mediation on your behalf.

Mediation will be conducted somewhere in your school district by a state-appointed mediator. These professionals are trained in dispute resolution and are often very helpful. Besides the Mediator, Mediation will likely include a supervisor or Director of Special Services, the case manager, and perhaps other staff who might offer information such as a teacher or CST member. If you have an attorney, your attorney will be handling all of this for you. If you do not have an attorney, I highly recommend you do not attend by yourself. Bring a spouse, a family member, or a trusted friend.

---

[32] "Insanity is doing the same thing over and over again, but expecting different results." Wrongly attributed to Albert Einstein, this line is from a book by mystery novelist Rita Mae Brown.

When Mediation commences, the Mediator will explain that Mediation is an attempt to resolve the dispute before it goes to a hearing. The Mediator will advise that she cannot force anyone to agree, that she will not keep her notes after the Mediation, and that she cannot be called to give evidence at a hearing. Those procedures are to help both sides think expansively of ways in which the dispute can be resolved. The Mediator will have everyone sign a participation sheet as she is talking.

When the Mediator concludes her remarks, she will turn to your attorney, or to you if you have no attorney. Since you were the party who filed for Mediation, you will have the first opportunity to speak. You should be prepared to give your opening statement. Write it out in advance. Be familiar with it so you can give it with appropriate smooth flow and emphasis, but you can read it to make sure you say everything you need to. Remember to stick to the facts. Explain briefly what the dispute is and how you would like it to be resolved.

Once you are finished speaking, the district will have an opportunity to speak. They may have their lawyer there to do the presentation. If that is the case, do not be afraid. The Mediator is there to ensure fairness in the proceeding. You should not interrupt when the district is speaking. If you have any thoughts or disagree with what was said, write it down.

When the district has made its presentation, the Mediator will likely separate the parties into two rooms. This is called caucusing. The Mediator will likely speak to you privately to determine what you might be willing to settle for. Then she will go and speak separately to the district staff. She may go back and forth between you and the district several times in order to try and reach a settlement. If that occurs, she will write up a formal mediation agreement which you and the district will sign.

If Mediation Fails

If your school district refuses to settle at Mediation, the Mediator will schedule you for a settlement conference with a judge or an actual hearing depending on your state process. Make sure to speak with your Mediator about this so you are clear on what to expect in your state.

At this point, if you do not have one already, I strongly suggest you contact an attorney immediately. Make sure you find an attorney who has years of experience in special education matters. In my law firm, in addition to their legal acumen, all of our attorneys have previous experience in other aspects of special education. Some of us have prior credentials as certified teachers of the handicapped (i.e., special education teachers), speech-and-language pathologists, school board attorneys, a licensed clinical social worker, and certified school social worker.

Tell whoever answers the phone that you are calling for an initial consultation and that your Mediation just ended unsuccessfully. The right attorney will understand the importance of this information.

If you receive a Notice of Hearing with a date for a hearing which falls before the date of your initial consultation with an attorney, contact the number on the Notice and request an adjournment so that you can consult legal counsel.

When you go for your initial consultation, make sure you bring all of your child's records for the attorney to review, including

127

the most recent IEP, all of your child's CST evaluations (or at least the last two sets so the attorney can compare for progress or regression), your Mediation and Due Process request and the district's Answer. All of these items should already be in your organizational binder, so bring the entire binder with you.

CHAPTER TWELVE
Message of Hope

If you are feeling overwhelmed by the tasks in front of you, remember:

- Rome wasn't built in a day.
- You have enough time to get this done.
- Focus on one day at a time.

Even if you have no religious belief or a different belief, you may be uplifted and comforted by this verse which I was given years ago. It gave me hope and courage as a single parent working my way through university. May it uplift you to new heights as well:

> "Be strong and courageous and get to work. Do not be frightened by the size of the task, for the Lord my God is with you. He will not forsake you. He will see to it that everything is finished correctly. 1 Chronicles 28:20.

Now that you know these legal principles, commonsense ideas, and therapeutic techniques, you are poised to create and develop engaging relationships with your child's school staff, and to have regular and successful meetings with your child's educational team. If and when disputes arise, you now have the tools to maintain your cool confidence and unflappable demeanor. You will gain respect and possibly develop life-long close relationships with the sincere and decent professionals who labor tirelessly on behalf of students all over this wonderful nation, but especially in your local school district. And you will achieve what you set out to do: ensure that your child is taught and learns the educational methods and tools for success, with all appropriate opportunities for as much post-secondary education, employment, and independence as possible.

We go forward!

Bibliography

To find information on Early Intervention:

https://www.cdc.gov/ncbddd/actearly/parents/states.html#t extlinks

Resources to learn when children should reach developmental milestones:

www.cdc.gov; www.marchofdimes.org; www.developingchild.harvard.edu; National Library of Medicine at www.nlm.nih.gov.

To review the federal law of IDEA, now re-codified as IDEIA, visit:

www.sites.ed.gov.

See www.fclawlib.libguides.com for a survey of 50 state special education laws and regulations.

You can read more about IEP's at this website:

https://www2.ed.gov/parents/needs/speced/iepguide/index. html

Find successful visualization techniques:

www.woopmylife.org

https://www.youtube.com/watch?v=YFImv3izCzE#:~:text= 5%20Powerful%20visualisation%20techniques%20Think%20a

bout%20this%3A%20everything,human%20creation%20exists
%20first%20in%20our...%20Skip%20navigation

https://www.youtube.com/watch?v=3ECTX18pBDM

Learn Emotional Freedom Tapping or EFT:

https://www.bing.com/videos/search?q=youtube+emotional
+freedom+techniques+%26+tapping+instruction&docid=608
024668823751652&mid=ABCD22D965E488A3DA4EABCD
22D965E488A3DA4E&view=detail&FORM=VIRE

You Are Invited!

For more than 40 years, the attorneys at Jayne Wesler's law firm, **Sussan Greenwald & Wesler**, have helped parents of children with special needs to manage issues from academic struggles to anxiety and behavioral disorders to life-threatening allergies. **If you need assistance, contact them today at 609-409-3500.**

Send me a friend request on FaceBook at Parents of Kids with Learning Challenges.

Sign up for Live SGW Q&A Town Halls or view the recorded videos at www.sgwlawfirm.com.

The attorneys at **Sussan Greenwald & Wesler** are available to speak to your group on a variety of topics, including:

- The Essentials of Special Education Law

- Transitioning from Early Intervention to Preschool – What Every Parent Needs to Know

- The Top Ten Mistakes Parents Make at IEP Meetings

- Bullying

- Comprehensive Estate Planning for Your Family Member with Special Needs

- The DDD Application Process, School Avoidance and Refusal

Contact us today at 609-409-3500 or via email through our website.

If your child is struggling, don't let another day go by while you watch and wait. The most difficult part is making that first phone call. Take that first step today to get your child the assistance she needs.

Do not underestimate the power of you!

Made in the USA
Monee, IL
19 February 2021